ENGLISH
FOR EVERYONE

PRACTICE BOOK LEVEL ❶

BUSINESS ENGLISH

FREE AUDIO
website and app
www.dkefe.com

Authors

Thomas Booth worked for 10 years as an English-language teacher in Poland and Russia. He now lives in England, where he works as an editor and English-language materials writer, notably of course books and vocabulary textbooks.

Trish Burrow worked for seven years as a teacher and teacher trainer in Poland and UK summer schools. After a year working in a UK college as an ELT lecturer, she worked as an editor of exams materials and then English-language teaching materials. She lives in the UK and is a freelance writer and editor.

Course consultant

Tim Bowen has taught English and trained teachers in more than 30 countries worldwide. He is the co-author of works on pronunciation teaching and language-teaching methodology, and author of numerous books for English-language teachers. He is currently a freelance materials writer, editor, and translator. He is a member of the Chartered Institute of Linguists.

Language consultant

Professor Susan Barduhn is an experienced English-language teacher, teacher trainer, and author, who has contributed to numerous publications. In addition to directing English-language courses in at least four different continents, she has been President of the International Association of Teachers of English as a Foreign Language, and an adviser to the British Council and the US State Department. She is currently a Professor at the School for International Training in Vermont, USA.

ENGLISH
FOR EVERYONE

PRACTICE BOOK LEVEL 1

BUSINESS ENGLISH

DK | Penguin Random House

Project Editors Lili Bryant, Laura Sandford
Art Editors Chrissy Barnard, Paul Drislane, Michelle Staples
Editor Ben Ffrancon Davies
Editorial Assistants Sarah Edwards, Helen Leech
Illustrators Edwood Burn, Michael Parkin, Gus Scott
Managing Editor Daniel Mills
Managing Art Editor Anna Hall
Audio Recording Manager Christine Stroyan
Jacket Designer Ira Sharma
Jacket Editor Claire Gell
Managing Jacket Editor Saloni Singh
Jacket Design Development Manager Sophia MTT
Producer, Pre-production Andy Hilliard
Producer Mary Slater
Publisher Andrew Macintyre
Art Director Karen Self
Publishing Director Jonathan Metcalf

DK India
Senior Managing Art Editor Arunesh Talapatra
Senior Art Editor Chhaya Sajwan
Art Editors Meenal Goel, Roshni Kapur
Assistant Art Editor Rohit Dev Bhardwaj
Illustrators Manish Bhatt, Arun Pottirayil, Sachin Tanwar, Mohd Zishan
Editorial Coordinator Priyanka Sharma
Pre-production Manager Balwant Singh
Senior DTP Designers Harish Aggarwal, Vishal Bhatia
DTP Designer Jaypal Chauhan

First published in Great Britain in 2017 by
Dorling Kindersley Limited
DK, One Embassy Gardens, 8 Viaduct Gardens,
London, SW11 7BW

The authorised representative in the EEA is
Dorling Kindersley Verlag GmbH. Arnulfstr. 124,
80636 Munich, Germany

A CIP catalogue record for this book
is available from the British Library.
ISBN: 978-0-2412-5372-4

Printed and bound in China

www.dk.com

MIX
Paper | Supporting
responsible forestry
FSC™ C018179

This book was made with Forest
Stewardship Council™ certified
paper – one small step in DK's
commitment to a sustainable future.
Learn more at
www.dk.com/uk/information/sustainability

Contents

How the course works

English for Everyone is designed for people who want to teach themselves the English language. The Business English edition covers essential English phrases and constructions for a wide range of common business scenarios.

Unlike other courses, *English for Everyone* uses images and graphics in all its learning and practice, to help you understand and remember as easily as possible. The practice book is packed with exercises designed to reinforce the lessons you have learned in the course book. Work through the units in order, making full use of the audio available on the website and app.

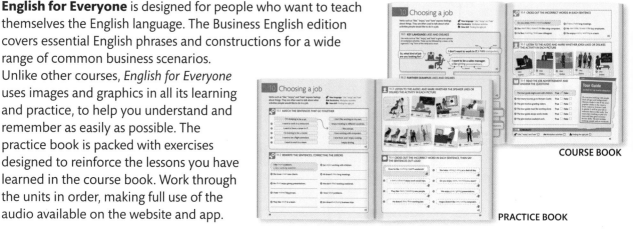

COURSE BOOK

PRACTICE BOOK

Unit number The book is divided into units. Each practice book unit tests the language taught in the course book unit with the same number.

Practice points Every unit begins with a summary of the key practice points.

Modules Each unit is broken down into modules, which should be done in order. You can take a break from learning after completing any module.

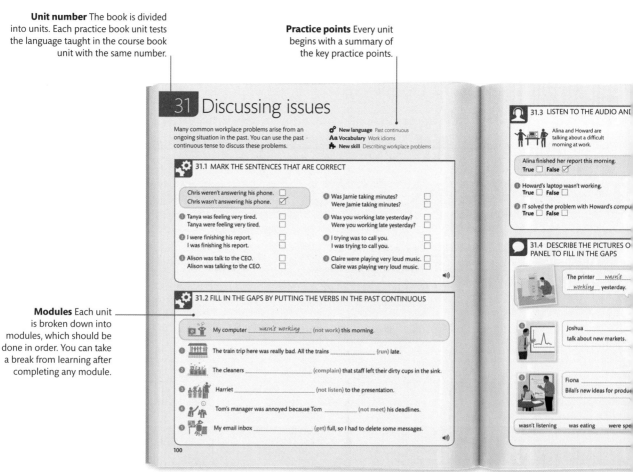

Vocabulary Throughout the book, vocabulary pages test your memory of key business English words and phrases taught in the course book.

Visual practice Images act as visual cues to help fix the most useful and important English words and phrases in your memory.

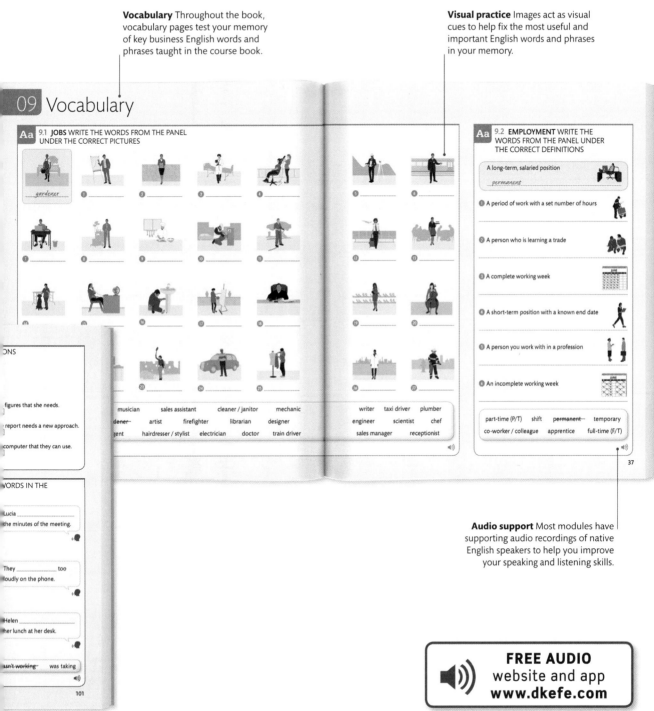

Audio support Most modules have supporting audio recordings of native English speakers to help you improve your speaking and listening skills.

FREE AUDIO
website and app
www.dkefe.com

Practice modules

Each exercise is carefully graded to drill and test the language taught in the corresponding course book units. Working through the exercises alongside the course book will help you remember what you have learned and become more fluent. Every exercise is introduced with a symbol to indicate which skill is being practiced.

 GRAMMAR
Apply new language rules in different contexts.

 READING
Examine target language in real-life English contexts.

 LISTENING
Test your understanding of spoken English.

 VOCABULARY
Cement your understanding of key vocabulary.

 SPEAKING
Compare your spoken English to model audio recordings.

Module number Every module is identified with a unique number, so you can easily locate answers and related audio.

Exercise instruction Every exercise is introduced with a brief instruction, telling you what you need to do.

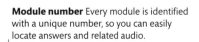 6.2 REWRITE THE STATEMENTS AS QUESTIONS

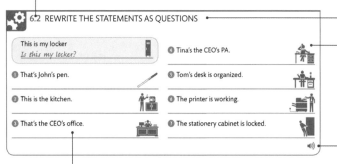

This is my locker
Is this my locker?

1 That's John's pen.
2 This is the kitchen.
3 That's the CEO's office.
4 Tina's the CEO's PA.
5 Tom's desk is organized.
6 The printer is working.
7 The stationery cabinet is locked.

Supporting graphics Visual cues are given to help you understand the exercises.

Supporting audio This symbol shows that the answers to the exercise are available as audio tracks. Listen to them after completing the exercise.

Space for writing You are encouraged to write your answers in the book for future reference.

Speaking exercise This symbol indicates that you should say your answers out loud, then compare them to model recordings included in your audio files.

Listening exercise This symbol indicates that you should listen to an audio track in order to answer the questions in the exercise.

Sample answer The first question of each exercise is answered for you, to help make the task easy to understand.

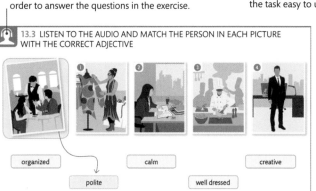 13.3 LISTEN TO THE AUDIO AND MATCH THE PERSON IN EACH PICTURE WITH THE CORRECT ADJECTIVE

organized
calm
creative
polite
well dressed

 6.8 SAY THE QUESTIONS OUT LOUD, FILLING IN THE GAPS USING THE WORDS IN THE PANEL

How do you get to work?

1 _____ buys the tea and coffee?
2 _____ is the printer not working?
3 _____ does the office open?
4 _____ do you want for lunch?
5 _____ is the meeting room?
6 _____ does the projector work?
7 _____ is the photocopier code?

| What | Where | How | Why |
| How | What | When | Who |

Audio

English for Everyone features extensive supporting audio materials. You are encouraged to use them as much as you can, to improve your understanding of spoken English, and to make your own accent and pronunciation more natural. Each file can be played, paused, and repeated as often as you like, until you are confident you understand what has been said.

LISTENING EXERCISES
This symbol indicates that you should listen to an audio track in order to answer the questions in the exercise.

SUPPORTING AUDIO
This symbol indicates that extra audio material is available for you to listen to after completing the module.

FREE AUDIO
website and app
www.dkefe.com

Answers

An answers section at the back of the book lists the correct answers for every exercise. Turn to these pages whenever you finish a module and compare your answers with the samples provided, to see how well you have understood each teaching point.

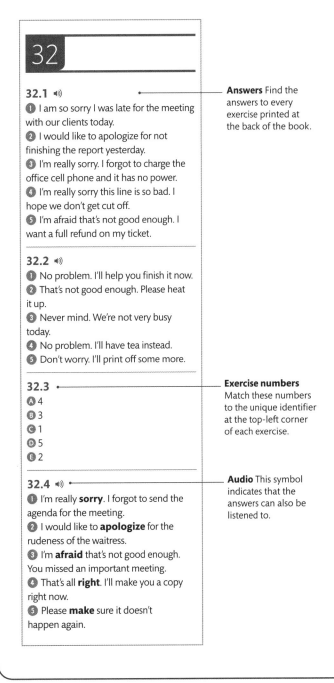

32

32.1 ◀))
❶ I am so sorry I was late for the meeting with our clients today.
❷ I would like to apologize for not finishing the report yesterday.
❸ I'm really sorry. I forgot to charge the office cell phone and it has no power.
❹ I'm really sorry this line is so bad. I hope we don't get cut off.
❺ I'm afraid that's not good enough. I want a full refund on my ticket.

Answers Find the answers to every exercise printed at the back of the book.

32.2 ◀))
❶ No problem. I'll help you finish it now.
❷ That's not good enough. Please heat it up.
❸ Never mind. We're not very busy today.
❹ No problem. I'll have tea instead.
❺ Don't worry. I'll print off some more.

32.3
Ⓐ 4
Ⓑ 3
Ⓒ 1
Ⓓ 5
Ⓔ 2

Exercise numbers Match these numbers to the unique identifier at the top-left corner of each exercise.

32.4 ◀))
❶ I'm really **sorry**. I forgot to send the agenda for the meeting.
❷ I would like to **apologize** for the rudeness of the waitress.
❸ I'm **afraid** that's not good enough. You missed an important meeting.
❹ That's all **right**. I'll make you a copy right now.
❺ Please **make** sure it doesn't happen again.

Audio This symbol indicates that the answers can also be listened to.

Meeting new colleagues

You can use formal or informal English to introduce yourself and greet colleagues or co-workers, depending on the situation and the people you are meeting.

New language Alphabet and spelling
Aa Vocabulary Introductions and greetings
New skill Introducing yourself to co-workers

1.1 MARK THE SENTENCES THAT ARE CORRECT

It's pleasure to meet you. ☐
It's a pleasure to meet you. ☑

1. My name Ali Patel. ☐
   My name's Ali Patel. ☐

2. Hi, I'm Jeff. ☐
   Hi, I Jeff. ☐

3. It good to meet you, Jane. ☐
   It's good to meet you, Jane. ☐

4. Pleased to meet you. ☐
   Please to meet you. ☐

5. I'm name is Deepak Kaur. ☐
   My name is Deepak Kaur. ☐

6. Great to meet you, Tanya. ☐
   Pleasure to meet you, Tanya. ☐

7. It's nice to meet you, too. ☐
   It's nice meet you, too. ☐

8. Good hello. My name is Ben Lewis. ☐
   Good morning. My name is Ben Lewis. ☐

9. It's a great to meet you, Gill. ☐
   It's great to meet you, Gill. ☐

10. Good evening. My name is Karen. ☐
    Great evening. My name is Karen. ☐

🔊

1.2 REWRITE THE SENTENCES, PUTTING THE WORDS IN THE CORRECT ORDER

name | afternoon. | is | Good | Tom. | My

Good afternoon. My name is Tom.

1. my | Hill. | Fiona | name's | Hello,

_____

2. too. | Nice | you, | meet | to

_____

3. good | Jim. | you, | to | It's | meet

_____

4. meet | Pleased | you. | to

_____

5. a | to | meet | It's | you. | pleasure

_____

6. name | Good | is | My | Roy. | evening.

_____

🔊

1.3 LISTEN TO THE AUDIO AND MARK THE NAMES THAT ARE SPELLED OUT

George — A
Jorge — B

1. Jayne — A / Jane — B
2. Adam — A / Alan — B
3. Sarah — A / Saleh — B
4. Mick — A / Mike — B
5. Carrie — A / Kerry — B

1.4 SPELL THE NAMES OUT LOUD

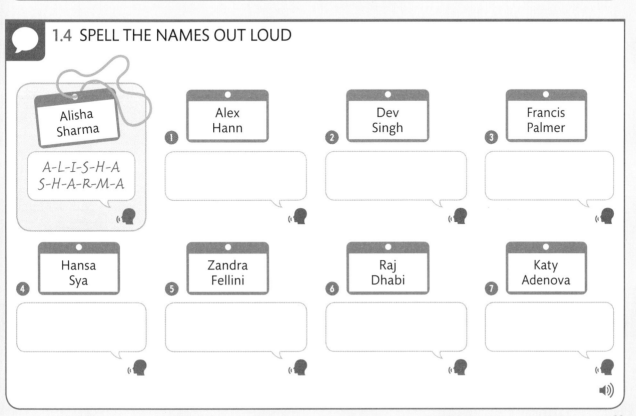

Alisha Sharma
A-L-I-S-H-A
S-H-A-R-M-A

1. Alex Hann
2. Dev Singh
3. Francis Palmer
4. Hansa Sya
5. Zandra Fellini
6. Raj Dhabi
7. Katy Adenova

13

1.5 REWRITE THE SENTENCES, CORRECTING THE ERRORS

> May you introduce Amy Daniels?
> _May I introduce Amy Daniels?_

1 This our new designer.

_____

2 Raj and I works together.

_____

3 I like you to meet our CEO.

_____

4 Hi, I'm name's Lola.

_____

5 It's great to meet to you, Emily.

_____

6 I may introduce Ewan Carlton?

_____

7 Farah, this my colleague, Leon.

_____

◀))

1.6 CROSS OUT THE INCORRECT WORD IN EACH SENTENCE

> Hi, Luke. This is / ~~meet~~ Emiko.

1 Good morning. I'm / My name's Saira Khan.

2 Bye / I'm Harry.

3 I'm / I's Andrew Shaw.

4 It's / It good to meet you.

5 Pleased to / I meet you.

6 It's a pleased / pleasure to meet you.

7 May / This I introduce our new HR assistant?

8 Keira, meets / meet John.

9 Great / Greater to meet you.

10 I would / had like you to meet Dan.

11 Colin and I works / work together.

◀))

1.7 LISTEN TO THE AUDIO, THEN NUMBER THE SENTENCES IN THE ORDER YOU HEAR THEM

Julia has recently started a new job. She meets some of her new co-workers at a company party.

A Meet Jim. He's our CEO. ☐

B It's nice to meet you, Julia. ☐

C Hi, Jim. It's great to meet you, too. ☐

D And this is Gary, our Marketing Manager. ☐

E May I introduce Julia Parker? ☐ 1

F It's a pleasure to meet you, too, Claire. ☐

G Pleased to meet you, Julia. ☐

02 Everyday work activities

Use the present simple to talk about things that you do regularly, such as your daily tasks or everyday work routines.

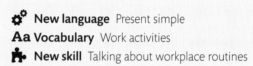

⚙ **New language** Present simple
Aa Vocabulary Work activities
🧩 **New skill** Talking about workplace routines

2.1 MATCH THE PICTURES TO THE CORRECT SENTENCES

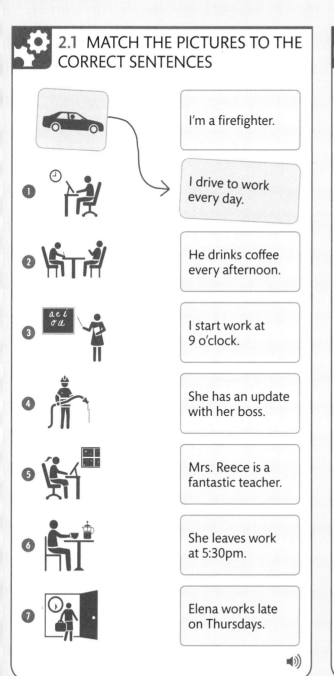

I'm a firefighter.

I drive to work every day.

He drinks coffee every afternoon.

I start work at 9 o'clock.

She has an update with her boss.

Mrs. Reece is a fantastic teacher.

She leaves work at 5:30pm.

Elena works late on Thursdays.

2.2 REWRITE THE SENTENCES, CORRECTING THE ERRORS

I be a teaching assistant at the local school.
I'm a teaching assistant at the local school.

1 The IT Helpdesk **are** really good.

_____

2 She **work** in a car factory.

_____

3 I **eating** my lunch in the park.

_____

4 We **takes** a break at 11am.

_____

5 John **write** the minutes of our meetings.

_____

6 Mrs. Rae **cleaning** the meeting rooms.

_____

7 The CEO **bring** cake on his birthday.

_____

8 I **prepares** presentations.

_____

9 Jomir **stop** for tea at 3pm.

_____

2.3 MARK THE SENTENCES THAT ARE CORRECT

The office close at 7 o'clock. ☐
The office closes at 7 o'clock. ☑

1 The CEO arrive at work early. ☐
The CEO arrives at work early. ☐

2 We have a hot-desking policy. ☐
We has a hot-desking policy. ☐

3 My assistant opens my mail. ☐
My assistant open my mail. ☐

4 Shazia be an engineer. ☐
Shazia is an engineer. ☐

5 Hal working for his uncle. ☐
Hal works for his uncle. ☐

6 I start work at 8:30am. ☐
I starts work at 8:30am. ☐

7 They finish at 5pm. ☐
They finishes at 5pm. ☐

8 They eating lunch in the cafeteria. ☐
They eat lunch in the cafeteria. ☐

9 Kate only drinks coffee. ☐
Kate only drink coffee. ☐

10 I calls the US office every Monday. ☐
I call the US office every Monday. ☐

11 Andrew helps me with my PC. ☐
Andrew help me with my PC. ☐

12 I replies to emails at 11am and 3pm. ☐
I reply to emails at 11am and 3pm. ☐

◀))

2.4 LISTEN TO THE AUDIO AND ANSWER THE QUESTIONS

Sarah's manager tells her what a typical day in her new job is like.

What happens at 9 o'clock?
The office opens ☐
The team starts work ☑
Sarah makes coffee ☐

1 Who makes the coffee at break time?
Sales staff ☐
Sales clients ☐
The manager's PA ☐

2 When do staff call clients?
At break time ☐
Before the break ☐
After the break ☐

3 How long can Sarah take for lunch?
An hour ☐
An hour and a half ☐
Two hours ☐

4 What time can Sarah take her lunch break?
11:30am ☐
12:30pm ☐
2:30pm ☐

5 What does the tech team do?
They call sales ☐
They analyze sales ☐
They make sales ☐

6 How often do staff get training?
Once a week ☐
Twice a week ☐
Three times a week ☐

2.5 CROSS OUT THE INCORRECT WORD IN EACH SENTENCE

Samia **takes** / ~~take~~ notes in our meetings.

❶ The director **has** / **haves** an open door policy.

❷ I **deal** / **deals** with all his emails.

❸ Gavin **leaves** / **leave** work at 7pm.

❹ They **works** / **work** evenings and weekends.

❺ She **ride** / **rides** her bike to work.

❻ Tim and Pat **bring** / **brings** their own lunch.

❼ Deepak **turn** / **turns** off his phone after work.

❽ Sobek and Kurt **plays** / **play** tennis after work.

❾ My boss **plan** / **plans** my work for the week.

2.6 SAY THE SENTENCES OUT LOUD, FILLING IN THE GAPS USING THE WORDS IN THE PANEL

I _____*write*_____ a list of my tasks every day.

❶ Lulu always _____ to work early.

❷ Our reps _____ clients at their office.

❸ The CEO _____ to all new staff.

❹ He's a nurse and he _____ weekends.

❺ Imran _____ with all the contracts.

❻ The printer _____ working late in the day.

❼ The staff _____ to a nearby café for lunch.

❽ Raj _____ a break at 11am.

❾ Sophie _____ a travel agent.

| deals | | go | | meet | | stops | | takes |
| talks | | gets | | ~~write~~ | | works | | is |

17

Aa 3.1 COUNTRIES AND CONTINENTS WRITE THE WORDS FROM THE PANEL UNDER THE CORRECT PICTURES

Poland

1 _____

2 _____

3 _____

4 _____

10 _____

11 _____

12 _____

13 _____

14 _____

20 _____

21 _____

22 _____

23 _____

24 _____

30 _____

31 _____

32 _____

33 _____

34 _____

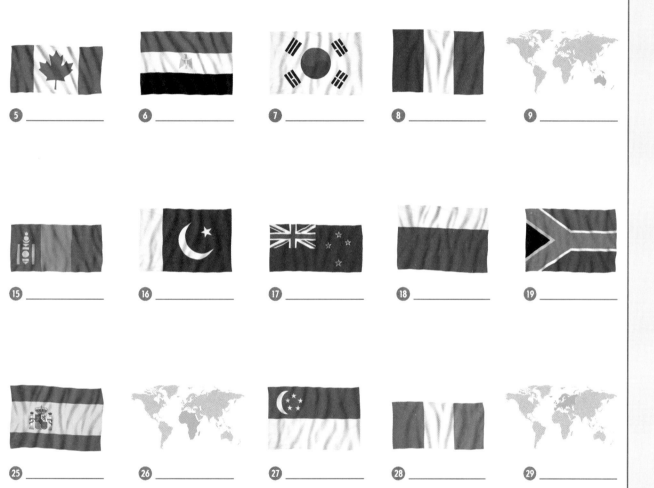

5 _____

6 _____

7 _____

8 _____

9 _____

15 _____

16 _____

17 _____

18 _____

19 _____

25 _____

26 _____

27 _____

28 _____

29 _____

Canada   Netherlands   Thailand   China   Japan   ~~Poland~~   Russia   India   Singapore

Mexico   Australia   New Zealand   Spain   France   Brazil   Asia   Africa   Germany   Europe

South Africa   Turkey   Argentina   Australasia   North America   Egypt   South Korea

South America   Austria   United States of America (US / USA)   Republic of Ireland (ROI)   Switzerland

United Kingdom (UK)   Pakistan   Mongolia   United Arab Emirates (UAE)

Business around the world

English uses "from" or nationality adjectives to talk about where products or people come from. "From" can also refer to your company or department.

⚙ **New language** Negative statements
Aa Vocabulary Countries and nationalities
🧩 **New skill** Saying where things are from

Aa 4.1 FIND FIVE MORE COUNTRIES IN THE GRID THAT MATCH THE FLAGS

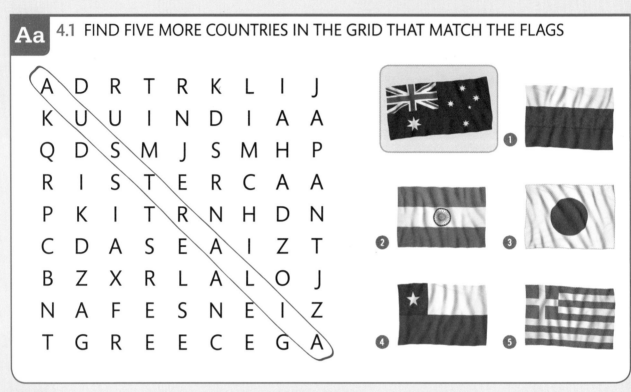

A	D	R	T	R	K	L	I	J
K	U	U	I	N	D	I	A	A
Q	D	S	M	J	S	M	H	P
R	I	S	T	E	R	C	A	A
P	K	I	T	R	N	H	D	N
C	D	A	S	E	A	I	Z	T
B	Z	X	R	L	A	L	O	J
N	A	F	E	S	N	E	I	Z
T	G	R	E	E	C	E	G	A

1
2
3
4
5

Aa 4.2 WRITE THE WORDS FROM THE PANEL IN THE CORRECT GROUPS

COUNTRIES

South Africa

NATIONALITIES

Brazilian

France ~~South Africa~~ British Greek Italy Canadian
Vietnam Japanese Switzerland ~~Brazilian~~ Spanish China

4.3 REWRITE EACH SENTENCE IN ITS OTHER FORM

| These new tablets are from China. | These new tablets are Chinese. |

1. _____ | The new CEO is Australian.
2. These new robots are from Japan. | _____
3. _____ | We sell Portuguese leather bags.
4. _____ | I'm Argentinian, but I work in the US.
5. The designer is from Britain. | _____
6. _____ | Our sales director is South Korean.
7. Our best-selling rugs are from India. | _____
8. _____ | These beautiful clothes are African.

🔊

4.4 MARK THE SENTENCES THAT ARE CORRECT

| Our restaurant serves Japan food. | ☐ |
| Our restaurant serves Japanese food. | ☑ |

1. Our CEO is America. ☐
   Our CEO is from America. ☐

2. I've got a flight to Italy next Monday. ☐
   I've got a flight to Italian next Monday. ☐

3. These sports cars are from French. ☐
   These sports cars are from France. ☐

4. Most of our fabrics are from Africa. ☐
   Most of our fabrics are from African. ☐

5. My PA is from Spanish. ☐
   My PA is from Spain. ☐

🔊

4.5 CROSS OUT THE INCORRECT WORD IN EACH SENTENCE

| Our best products are from Russia / ~~Russian~~. |

1. We sell smartphones from Japan / Japanese.
2. The HR manager is from America / American.
3. My team follows the China / Chinese markets.
4. Travel to the Greece / Greek islands with us.
5. Our products are from Vietnam / Vietnamese.
6. Our CEO is Canada / Canadian.
7. Most of the sales team is from Spain / Spanish.
8. I'm British, but I work in Italy / Italian.
9. I have a lot of Mexico / Mexican co-workers.
10. My new assistant is from France / French.

🔊

21

4.6 REWRITE THE SENTENCES, CORRECTING THE ERRORS USING SHORT FORMS

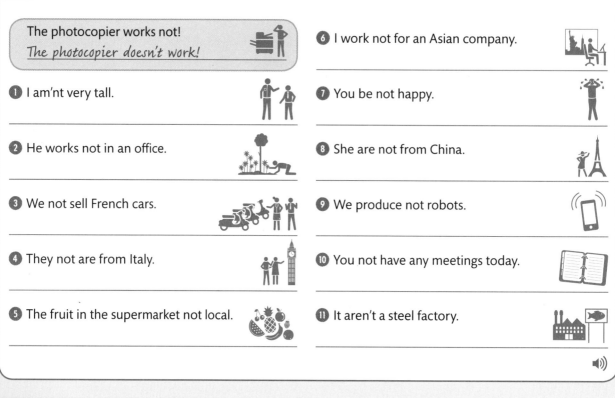

The photocopier works not!
The photocopier doesn't work!

❶ I am'nt very tall.

❷ He works not in an office.

❸ We not sell French cars.

❹ They not are from Italy.

❺ The fruit in the supermarket not local.

❻ I work not for an Asian company.

❼ You be not happy.

❽ She are not from China.

❾ We produce not robots.

❿ You not have any meetings today.

⓫ It aren't a steel factory.

4.7 SAY THE SENTENCES OUT LOUD, USING SHORT FORMS

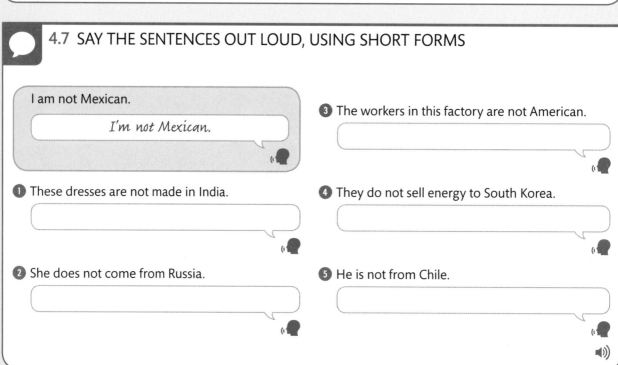

I am not Mexican.

I'm not Mexican.

❶ These dresses are not made in India.

❷ She does not come from Russia.

❸ The workers in this factory are not American.

❹ They do not sell energy to South Korea.

❺ He is not from Chile.

4.8 LISTEN TO THE AUDIO AND ANSWER THE QUESTIONS

Nadia, Tim, and Carlos are attending a conference.

What department does Nadia work in?
Finance ☐ Sales ☑ IT ☐

❶ What department does Carlos work in?
Finance ☐ Sales ☐ IT ☐

❷ Who hasn't Nadia met before?
Carlos ☐ Tim ☐ Neither of them ☐

❸ What department does Tim work in?
Finance ☐ Marketing ☐ IT ☐

❹ Who has to report back to their team?
Tim ☐ Nadia ☐ Carlos ☐

❺ Where will Tim's company launch a brand?
China ☐ Chile ☐ Japan ☐

4.9 READ THE ARTICLE AND ANSWER THE QUESTIONS

The company sells food from one country.
True ☐ False ☑ Not given ☐

❶ The CEO has visited many different countries.
True ☐ False ☐ Not given ☐

❷ He stayed with local people in each country.
True ☐ False ☐ Not given ☐

❸ All Fairtrade coffee comes from Chile.
True ☐ False ☐ Not given ☐

❹ Some Fairtrade products come from Kenya.
True ☐ False ☐ Not given ☐

❺ Food always tastes better if it's Fairtrade.
True ☐ False ☐ Not given ☐

❻ "Tasters" choose the food that the company sells.
True ☐ False ☐ Not given ☐

❼ "Selectors" find new foods to sell.
True ☐ False ☐ Not given ☐

Foods from around the World

Founded in 2005, Foods from around the World brings you food from every corner of the globe. Their CEO, Johnathon Medway, had the idea for the company after he spent a year traveling around the world, eating exotic foods in each country that he visited.

Johnathon says, "We buy directly from our producers and all the food you buy from us has the Fairtrade guarantee. That means the food is from small-scale farmers in countries like India, Chile, and Egypt. Workers are treated fairly and paid a living wage. So Costa Rican coffee growers and Kenyan tea growers all earn enough to live on if you buy our products."

So, how does the company find new products to sell? They have a team of "tasters" who travel around a different region of the world, trying food in markets, cafés, and from shops and factories. The "tasters" then make a shortlist of their favorite products for the "selectors" to choose from at the head office. Finally, the "selectors" talk to the producer and agree a trade deal. So, next time you want to eat something interesting, go to Foods from around the World.

05 Vocabulary

5.1 OFFICE EQUIPMENT WRITE THE WORDS FROM THE PANEL UNDER THE CORRECT PICTURES

photocopier

1 _____

2 _____

3 _____

4 _____

8 _____

9 _____

10 _____

11 _____

12 _____

16 _____

17 _____

18 _____

19 _____

20 _____

24 _____

25 _____

26 _____

27 _____

28 _____

5 _____

6 _____

7 _____

13 _____

14 _____

15 _____

21 _____

22 _____

23 _____

29 _____

30 _____

31 _____

letter   adhesive tape

planner (US) / diary (UK)   notepad

computer   pencil   ruler

files / folders   stapler

lamp   hole punch

pencil sharpener   highlighter

laptop   pen   chair

eraser (US) / rubber (UK)

calendar   paper clips   headset

rubber bands   shredder

~~photocopier~~   clipboard

hard drive   scanner

telephone / phone   projector

envelope   printer   tablet

cell phone (US) / mobile phone (UK)

🔊

It is important to use the correct word order and question words in English questions, depending on whether the questions are open-ended.

🔧 **New language** Forming questions
Aa Vocabulary Office equipment
🧩 **New skill** Asking colleagues questions

6.1 REWRITE THE QUESTIONS, PUTTING THE WORDS IN THE CORRECT ORDER

| this | Is | cafeteria? | the |

Is this the cafeteria?

1 | this | working? | printer | Is |

_____

2 | desk? | this | Is | your |

_____

3 | closed? | the | windows | Are |

_____

4 | this | locked? | Is | cupboard |

_____

5 | messy? | desk | his | Is |

_____

6 | CEO? | the | she | Is |

_____

7 | assistant? | Jo's | you | Are |

_____

🔊

6.2 REWRITE THE STATEMENTS AS QUESTIONS

This is my locker
Is this my locker?

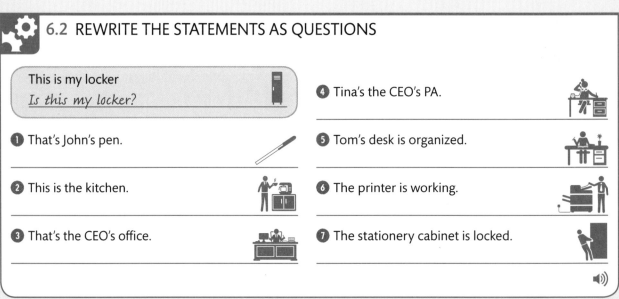

1 That's John's pen.

2 This is the kitchen.

3 That's the CEO's office.

4 Tina's the CEO's PA.

5 Tom's desk is organized.

6 The printer is working.

7 The stationery cabinet is locked.

🔊

6.3 FILL IN THE GAPS USING "DO" OR "DOES"

Does she come in at 9am?

1. _____ you have an appointment?
2. _____ she work with Justin?
3. _____ your office have a scanner?
4. _____ you go to the finance meetings?
5. _____ Kish write the minutes?
6. _____ you have a stapler I can borrow?
7. _____ Saul work in your team?
8. _____ they know what to do?
9. _____ he know the CEO?
10. _____ we have a meeting now?

🔊

6.4 LISTEN TO THE AUDIO AND ANSWER THE QUESTIONS

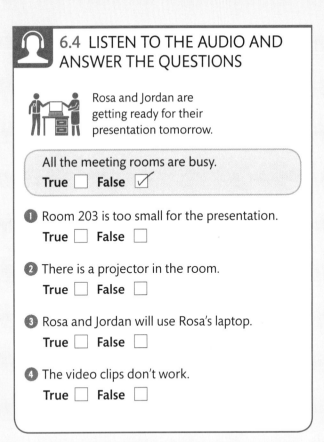

Rosa and Jordan are getting ready for their presentation tomorrow.

All the meeting rooms are busy.
True ☐ **False** ☑

1. Room 203 is too small for the presentation.
True ☐ **False** ☐

2. There is a projector in the room.
True ☐ **False** ☐

3. Rosa and Jordan will use Rosa's laptop.
True ☐ **False** ☐

4. The video clips don't work.
True ☐ **False** ☐

6.5 MATCH THE SITUATIONS TO THE CORRECT QUESTIONS

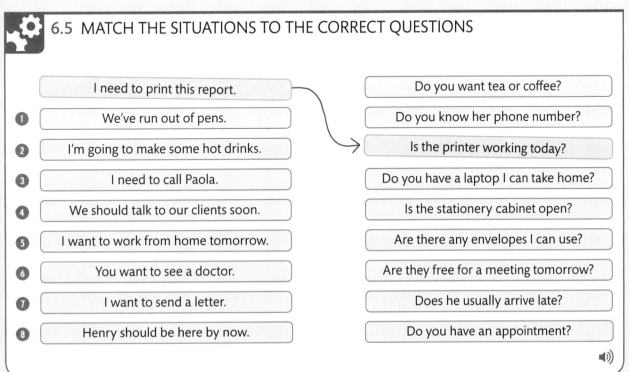

Situations	Questions
I need to print this report.	Do you want tea or coffee?
1. We've run out of pens.	Do you know her phone number?
2. I'm going to make some hot drinks.	Is the printer working today?
3. I need to call Paola.	Do you have a laptop I can take home?
4. We should talk to our clients soon.	Is the stationery cabinet open?
5. I want to work from home tomorrow.	Are there any envelopes I can use?
6. You want to see a doctor.	Are they free for a meeting tomorrow?
7. I want to send a letter.	Does he usually arrive late?
8. Henry should be here by now.	Do you have an appointment?

🔊

6.6 CROSS OUT THE INCORRECT WORD IN EACH QUESTION

Where / ~~Which~~ are you going on vacation?

❶ How / Who does the scanner work?

❷ What / When is on the agenda for the meeting?

❸ Who / Why is the stationery cabinet locked?

❹ Who / When do we have a break for lunch?

❺ Where / What is the CEO's office?

❻ When / What is the door code?

❼ What / Who do I ask for ink for the printer?

🔊

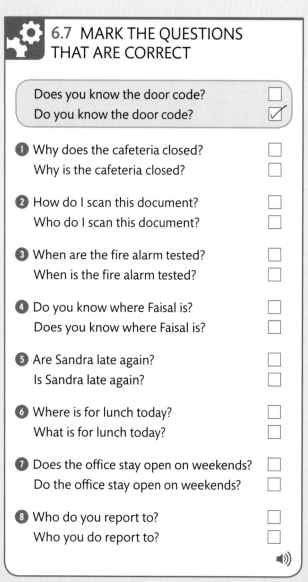

6.7 MARK THE QUESTIONS THAT ARE CORRECT

Does you know the door code? ☐
Do you know the door code? ☑

❶ Why does the cafeteria closed? ☐
Why is the cafeteria closed? ☐

❷ How do I scan this document? ☐
Who do I scan this document? ☐

❸ When are the fire alarm tested? ☐
When is the fire alarm tested? ☐

❹ Do you know where Faisal is? ☐
Does you know where Faisal is? ☐

❺ Are Sandra late again? ☐
Is Sandra late again? ☐

❻ Where is for lunch today? ☐
What is for lunch today? ☐

❼ Does the office stay open on weekends? ☐
Do the office stay open on weekends? ☐

❽ Who do you report to? ☐
Who you do report to? ☐

🔊

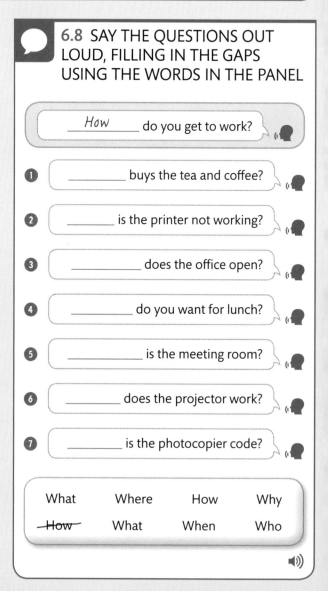

6.8 SAY THE QUESTIONS OUT LOUD, FILLING IN THE GAPS USING THE WORDS IN THE PANEL

___How___ do you get to work? 🗣

❶ _____ buys the tea and coffee? 🗣

❷ _____ is the printer not working? 🗣

❸ _____ does the office open? 🗣

❹ _____ do you want for lunch? 🗣

❺ _____ is the meeting room? 🗣

❻ _____ does the projector work? 🗣

❼ _____ is the photocopier code? 🗣

| What | Where | How | Why |
| ~~How~~ | What | When | Who |

🔊

28

Exchanging details

When making new business contacts, there are several phrases you can use to ask for their details and offer yours in return.

⚙ **New language** Short answers
Aa Vocabulary Contact information
New skill Exchanging contact details

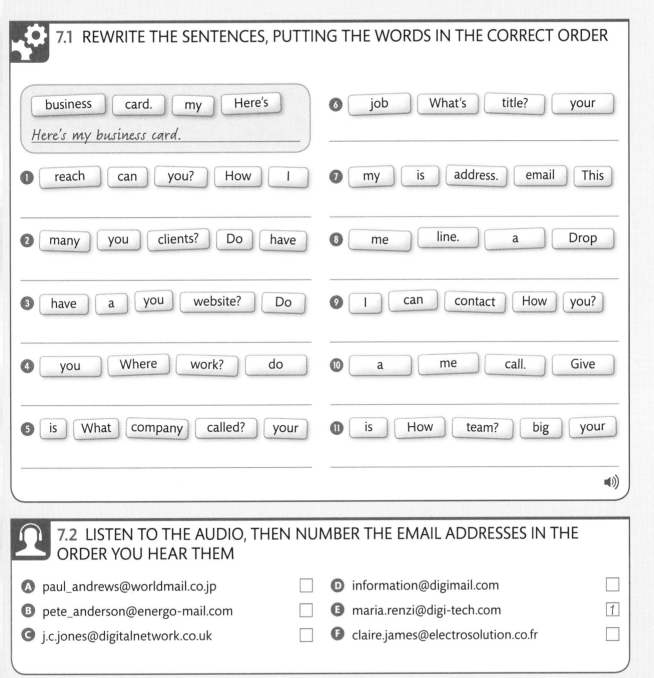

7.1 REWRITE THE SENTENCES, PUTTING THE WORDS IN THE CORRECT ORDER

| business | card. | my | Here's |

Here's my business card.

1 | reach | can | you? | How | I |

2 | many | you | clients? | Do | have |

3 | have | a | you | website? | Do |

4 | you | Where | work? | do |

5 | is | What | company | called? | your |

6 | job | What's | title? | your |

7 | my | is | address. | email | This |

8 | me | line. | a | Drop |

9 | I | can | contact | How | you? |

10 | a | me | call. | Give |

11 | is | How | team? | big | your |

7.2 LISTEN TO THE AUDIO, THEN NUMBER THE EMAIL ADDRESSES IN THE ORDER YOU HEAR THEM

A paul_andrews@worldmail.co.jp ☐

B pete_anderson@energo-mail.com ☐

C j.c.jones@digitalnetwork.co.uk ☐

D information@digimail.com ☐

E maria.renzi@digi-tech.com ☐ 1

F claire.james@electrosolution.co.fr ☐

7.3 CROSS OUT THE INCORRECT WORD IN EACH SENTENCE

Do you have a ~~email~~ / **business** card?

1 How can I **reach** / touch you for more information?

2 Drop me a **call** / line when you're visiting next.

3 Does your company keep / **have** a website?

4 Please stay in reach / **touch**.

5 Is this your **correct** / precise phone number?

6 Line / **Call** me if you want further details.

7 Is this your present / **current** email address?

8 My job **title** / name is on the business card.

9 Do you **have** / got a portfolio with you?

7.4 LOOK AT THE BUSINESS CARDS AND ANSWER THE QUESTIONS

Stronger Web Solutions is a café.
True ☐ **False** ☑ **Not given** ☐

1 Janice Strong is a web designer.
True ☐ **False** ☐ **Not given** ☐

2 Stronger Web Solutions has a website.
True ☐ **False** ☐ **Not given** ☐

3 Greybridge History Museum is 100 years old.
True ☐ **False** ☐ **Not given** ☐

4 Dan has a website.
True ☐ **False** ☐ **Not given** ☐

5 Dan works as an archaeologist.
True ☐ **False** ☐ **Not given** ☐

6 Dan has an email address.
True ☐ **False** ☐ **Not given** ☐

7 Paul is a web designer.
True ☐ **False** ☐ **Not given** ☐

8 Consoul is based in Los Angeles.
True ☐ **False** ☐ **Not given** ☐

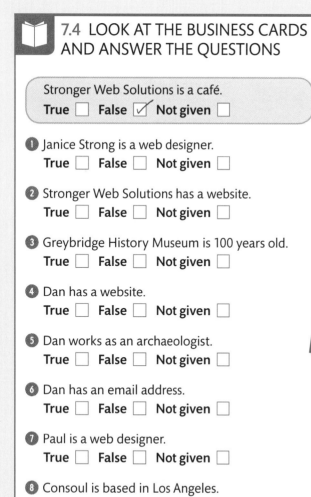

Janice Strong
Web Designer
www.strongerweb.com

STRONGER WEB SOLUTIONS
Tel: 1 (545) 345-2342
info@strongerweb.com

GREYBRIDGE HISTORY MUSEUM
Seal Street, Daltry, Hertfordshire, H23 9NB
Dan Stone - Historian
Email: dstone@greybridge.co.uk
Tel: 0743 235 436

CONSOUL
Managing consultant, ConSoul

PAUL@CONSOUL.COM
07853453452
23 Garden Walk
Cambridge
C43 7FD

7.5 MATCH THE SENTENCES TO THE CORRECT SHORT ANSWERS

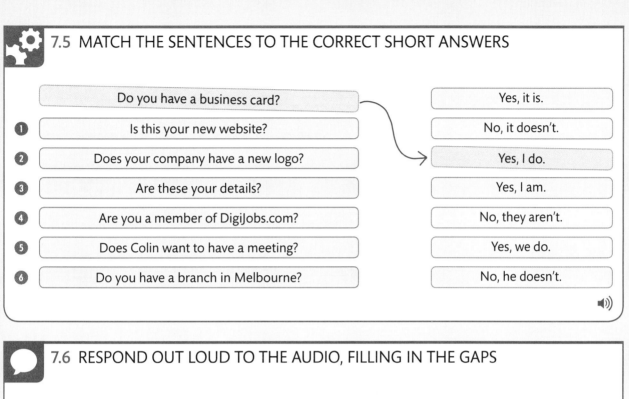

Do you have a business card?

Yes, it is.

1 Is this your new website?

No, it doesn't.

2 Does your company have a new logo?

Yes, I do.

3 Are these your details?

Yes, I am.

4 Are you a member of DigiJobs.com?

No, they aren't.

5 Does Colin want to have a meeting?

Yes, we do.

6 Do you have a branch in Melbourne?

No, he doesn't.

7.6 RESPOND OUT LOUD TO THE AUDIO, FILLING IN THE GAPS

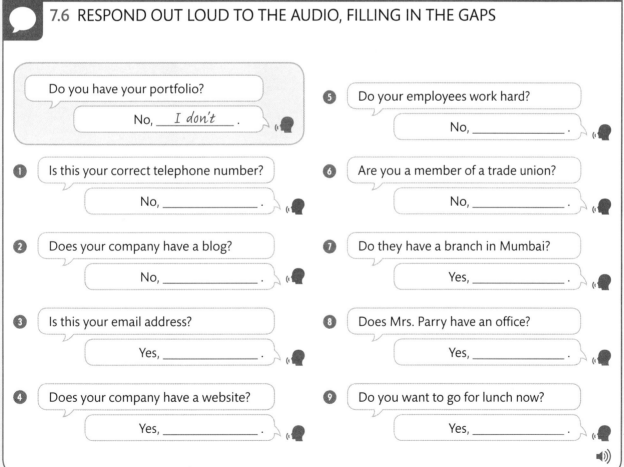

Do you have your portfolio?

No, _I don't_ .

1 Is this your correct telephone number?

No, _____ .

2 Does your company have a blog?

No, _____ .

3 Is this your email address?

Yes, _____ .

4 Does your company have a website?

Yes, _____ .

5 Do your employees work hard?

No, _____ .

6 Are you a member of a trade union?

No, _____ .

7 Do they have a branch in Mumbai?

Yes, _____ .

8 Does Mrs. Parry have an office?

Yes, _____ .

9 Do you want to go for lunch now?

Yes, _____ .

08 Skills and experience

English uses the verb "have" to talk about people's skills, experience, and professional attributes. You might also hear "have got" in informal UK English.

🔧 **New language** "Have," "have got," articles
Aa Vocabulary Jobs and skills
🧩 **New skill** Writing a business profile

8.1 CROSS OUT THE INCORRECT WORDS IN EACH SENTENCE

He doesn't have / ~~has~~ a typing qualification.

1 She have / has an excellent résumé.

2 I has / have good people skills.

3 They don't have / don't got much time.

4 Do you has / have previous experience?

5 He's got / haves excellent keyboard skills.

6 I doesn't have / don't have my own office.

7 Does he have / got any training?

8 They having / have a can-do outlook.

9 You don't have / hasn't his number, do you?

🔊

8.2 REWRITE THE SENTENCES, PUTTING THE WORDS IN THE CORRECT ORDER

| he | experience | this | Has | for | got | job? | enough |

Has he got enough experience for this job?

1 | degree | you | in | have | business? | Do | higher | a |

2 | Business | has | He | the | MBA | School. | from | Boston | an |

3 | receptionist. | don't | a | full-time | have | They |

4 | excellent | have | assistant | Does | résumé? | an | your |

🔊

32

Hamid Syal

SALES AND MARKETING PROFESSIONAL

Experience

I am a creative and proactive marketing professional who has varied experience in the travel industry. I love helping people realize their dreams of visiting new places and devising new ways to market vacations. I started work in the hotel industry as a receptionist before working my way up to deputy manager. I have worked in countries such as Japan, India, and South Africa and for well-known, prestigious hotels such as The Ritz. I have a passion for travel and often visit new countries. My next vacation is to Tanzania, where I hope to go on safari.

Achievements

- Advising Explore the World travel agency on how to grow new markets and existing ones.
- Investigating and taking forward new business ideas, providing strategic recommendations to the SMT (Senior Management Team).
- Acting as the public-facing representative of Safari Travels, giving presentations at industry events.

Skills

I have excellent people skills, learned from my time in the hotel sector.
I enjoy working in teams to market vacations on behalf of a wide range of clients.

Qualifications

- BS Business and Hospitality Management, London South Bank University, 2010
- Diploma in Marketing, CIM (Chartered Institute of Marketing), 2015

What job does Hamid have? **He's a sales rep** ☐ **He's the CEO** ☐ **He works in marketing** ☑

❶ What industry does Hamid work in? **Hotels** ☐ **Travel** ☐ **Airlines** ☐

❷ Where has Hamid worked before? **A department store** ☐ **A restaurant** ☐ **A hotel** ☐

❸ Who has Hamid advised on strategy? **Strategists** ☐ **Management** ☐ **The Chief Executive** ☐

❹ How does Hamid describe his people skills? **Average** ☐ **Good** ☐ **Excellent** ☐

❺ In what situation does Hamid say he enjoys working? **Alone** ☐ **In teams** ☐ **With clients** ☐

❻ What is the subject of Hamid's diploma? **Business** ☐ **Marketing** ☐ **Hospitality Management** ☐

8.4 MARK THE SENTENCES THAT ARE CORRECT

I have excellent interpersonal skills. ✓
I have excellent the interpersonal skills. ☐

1 The new chef is very talented. ☐
A new chef is very talented. ☐

2 Toby is a accountant. ☐
Toby is an accountant. ☐

3 Search engines are invaluable. ☐
The search engines are invaluable. ☐

4 She works for a leading company. ☐
She works for leading company. ☐

5 Have you seen an ad I told you about? ☐
Have you seen the ad I told you about? ☐

6 They are out of office. ☐
They are out of the office. ☐

7 Did you see the new designs? ☐
Did you see a new designs? ☐

8 They hired best candidate. ☐
They hired the best candidate. ☐

9 What skills does the job require? ☐
What a skills does the job require? ☐

10 Is there an office in India? ☐
Is there a office in India? ☐

11 I have the certificate in sales. ☐
I have a certificate in sales. ☐

12 He works for a biggest store. ☐
He works for the biggest store. ☐

13 Interns are only paid expenses. ☐
Interns are only paid the expenses. ☐

🔊

 8.5 FILL IN THE GAPS USING "A," "AN," OR "THE"

He works in ____*a*____ phone store.

1 I worked as _____ intern at Beales.

2 I know _____ café you mean.

3 There's ____ printer on the second floor.

4 Jon hasn't got _____ diploma.

5 The CEO is in _____ NY office this week.

6 He's _____ amazing architect.

7 I just started _____ new job.

8 I'd like to put _____ ad in the paper.

9 Have you read _____ job description?

10 I work at _____ theater next door.

11 _____ new café does great coffee.

12 Where is _____ presentation?

13 The Tate is _____ art gallery.

14 I like _____ new CEO.

🔊

34

8.6 LISTEN TO THE AUDIO, THEN NUMBER THE PICTURES IN THE ORDER THEY ARE DESCRIBED

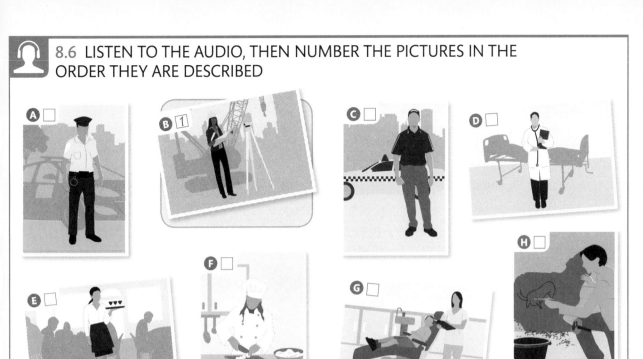

8.7 SAY THE SENTENCES OUT LOUD, CORRECTING THE ERRORS

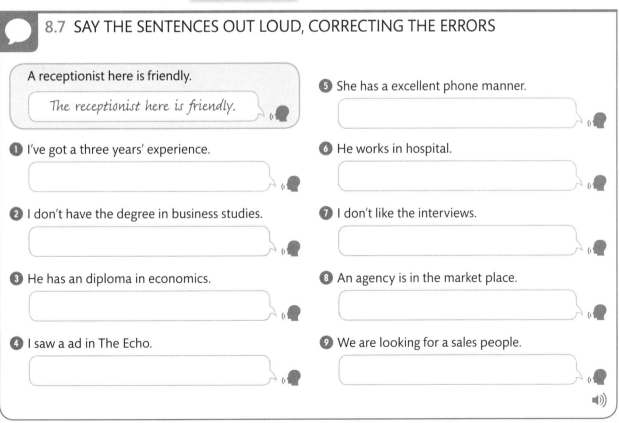

A receptionist here is friendly.

The receptionist here is friendly.

① I've got a three years' experience.

② I don't have the degree in business studies.

③ He has an diploma in economics.

④ I saw a ad in The Echo.

⑤ She has a excellent phone manner.

⑥ He works in hospital.

⑦ I don't like the interviews.

⑧ An agency is in the market place.

⑨ We are looking for a sales people.

09 Vocabulary

Aa 9.1 JOBS WRITE THE WORDS FROM THE PANEL UNDER THE CORRECT PICTURES

gardener

1 _____

2 _____

3 _____

4 _____

7 _____

8 _____

9 _____

10 _____

11 _____

14 _____

15 _____

16 _____

17 _____

18 _____

21 _____

22 _____

23 _____

24 _____

25 _____

tour guide	judge	musician	sales assistant	cleaner / janitor	mechanic
vet	surgeon	~~gardener~~	artist	firefighter	librarian	designer
waitress	pilot	travel agent	hairdresser / stylist	electrician	doctor	train driver

5 _____   6 _____

12 _____   13 _____

19 _____   20 _____

26 _____   27 _____

writer   taxi driver   plumber

engineer   scientist   chef

sales manager   receptionist

A long-term, salaried position

permanent

❶ A period of work with a set number of hours

_____

❷ A person who is learning a trade

_____

❸ A complete working week

_____

❹ A short-term position with a known end date

_____

❺ A person you work with in a profession

_____

❻ An incomplete working week

_____

part-time (P/T)   shift   ~~permanent~~   temporary

co-worker / colleague   apprentice   full-time (F/T)

10 Choosing a job

Verbs such as "like," "enjoy," and "hate" express feelings about things. They are often used to talk about what activities people would like to do in a job.

🔧 **New language** "Like," "enjoy," and "hate"
Aa Vocabulary Workplace activities
🧩 **New skill** Finding the right job

10.1 MATCH THE SENTENCES THAT GO TOGETHER

I'm studying to be a vet.	I don't like working on my own.
❶ I want to work in a restaurant.	I enjoy traveling to different countries.
❷ I want to have a career in IT.	I like animals.
❸ I'm training to be a courier.	I love working with computers.
❹ I want to be a flight attendant.	I love food, and I enjoy cooking.
❺ I want to work in a team.	I enjoy driving.

🔊

10.2 REWRITE THE SENTENCES, CORRECTING THE ERRORS

I like **work** outdoors.
I like working outdoors.

❶ She loves **meet** new clients.

_____

❷ He **don't** enjoy giving presentations.

_____

❸ I hate **trained** big groups.

_____

❹ They like **work** in a team.

_____

❺ Jan **enjoy** working with children.

_____

❻ Ali doesn't **likes** long meetings.

_____

❼ We don't **liked** working weekends.

_____

❽ I love **solve** problems.

_____

❾ Jim doesn't **enjoying** business trips.

_____

🔊

10.3 LISTEN TO THE AUDIO, AND MARK WHETHER THE SPEAKER LIKES OR DISLIKES THE ACTIVITY IN EACH PICTURE

Likes ✓   Dislikes ☐

① Likes ☐   Dislikes ☐

② Likes ☐   Dislikes ☐

③ Likes ☐   Dislikes ☐

④ Likes ☐   Dislikes ☐

⑤ Likes ☐   Dislikes ☐

⑥ Likes ☐   Dislikes ☐

⑦ Likes ☐   Dislikes ☐

10.4 CROSS OUT THE INCORRECT WORD IN EACH SENTENCE, THEN SAY THE SENTENCES OUT LOUD

Does he like working / ~~work~~ weekends?

① I don't / doesn't enjoy work social trips.

② They like meet / meeting new people.

③ He doesn't like / likes working late.

④ She hates sitting / siting at a desk all day.

⑤ Do you enjoy work / working in a team?

⑥ We enjoy give / giving presentations.

⑦ Angus doesn't like use / using computers.

11 Describing your workplace

One way of telling people about your company is by using "there is" and "there are." Use "Is there...?" or "Are there...?" to ask questions about a workplace.

⚙ **New language** "There is" and "there are"
Aa Vocabulary Office equipment
🧩 **New skill** Describing a workplace

11.1 MARK THE SENTENCES THAT ARE CORRECT

There is a washroom on this floor? ☐
Is there a washroom on this floor? ☑

❶ There are three printers in your department. ☐
There're three printers in your department. ☐

❷ Are there ladies' toilets on the second floor? ☐
Is there ladies' toilets on the second floor? ☐

❸ There isnt a cafeteria in the building. ☐
There isn't a cafeteria in the building. ☐

❹ Is there a set time for lunch breaks? ☐
Is there any set time for lunch breaks? ☐

❺ There are'nt any elevators in the office. ☐
There aren't any elevators in the office. ☐

❻ Is there a dress code at this company? ☐
Are there a dress code at this company? ☐

❼ There's photocopier on the first floor. ☐
There's a photocopier on the first floor. ☐

❽ There aren't a trash cans in the office. ☐
There aren't any trash cans in the office. ☐

❾ There are any interns on your team? ☐
Are there any interns on your team? ☐

❿ There is a calendar on the notice board. ☐
There are a calendar on the notice board. ☐

◀))

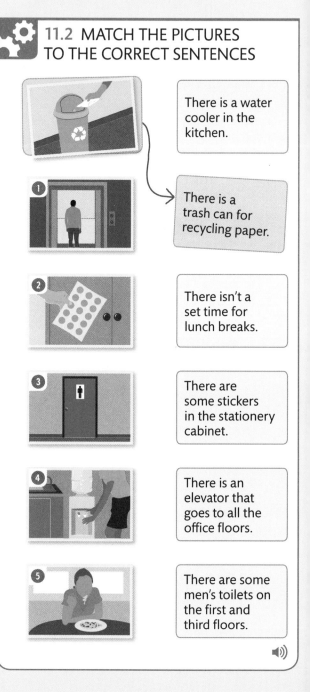

11.2 MATCH THE PICTURES TO THE CORRECT SENTENCES

There is a water cooler in the kitchen.

There is a trash can for recycling paper.

There isn't a set time for lunch breaks.

There are some stickers in the stationery cabinet.

There is an elevator that goes to all the office floors.

There are some men's toilets on the first and third floors.

◀))

40

11.3 LISTEN TO THE AUDIO AND ANSWER THE QUESTIONS

Debbie is telling Boris about her first day at her new job.

There are five people on Debbie's team.
True ☑ False ☐ Not given ☐

1 There is an elevator in Debbie's office.
True ☐ False ☐ Not given ☐

2 There isn't a separate office for Debbie's team.
True ☐ False ☐ Not given ☐

3 Debbie's office is on the third floor.
True ☐ False ☐ Not given ☐

4 There is a printer in Debbie's office.
True ☐ False ☐ Not given ☐

5 There is a casual dress code.
True ☐ False ☐ Not given ☐

6 There's a deli near the office.
True ☐ False ☐ Not given ☐

11.4 CROSS OUT THE INCORRECT WORD IN EACH SENTENCE, THEN SAY THE SENTENCES OUT LOUD

There is / are lots of great restaurants close to my office.

1 There is / are two positions available at our company.

2 There isn't a / any toaster in the kitchen, but there is a microwave.

3 Is / Are there a spare computer I can use?

4 Are there a / any pencils in the stationery cabinet?

5 There is / are a big meeting room in our new office.

12 Vocabulary

debit card

① _____

② _____

③ _____

④ _____

⑤ _____

⑥ _____

⑦ _____

⑧ _____

⑨ _____

⑩ _____

⑪ _____

⑫ _____

⑬ _____

⑭ _____

⑮ _____

currency	credit card	receipt	cash register (US) / till (UK)	debit card	bank
bills (US) / notes (UK)	invoice	cash machine / ATM	wallet	withdraw money
check (US) / cheque (UK)	online banking	safe	mobile banking	transfer money

42

Aa 12.2 PAY AND CONDITIONS WRITE THE WORDS FROM THE PANEL UNDER THE CORRECT DEFINITIONS

The amount of money paid per week or month

wage

❶ Additional pay for extra hours worked

_____

❷ A fixed, regular payment every month, often expressed as an annual sum

_____

❸ Extras given to employees in addition to their usual pay

_____

❹ An increase in pay

_____

❺ To receive money in return for labor or services

_____

❻ Money added to a person's wages as a reward for good performance

_____

❼ Paid time off work granted by employers

_____

❽ The amount of money paid per hour

_____

❾ A reduction in pay

_____

a bonus	salary	annual vacation (US) / annual leave (UK)	a pay cut	~~wage~~
to earn	hourly rate	overtime	a raise (US) / a pay rise (UK)	benefits

13 Personal qualities

You will encounter people with different skills and personalities at work. It is useful to be able to describe your co-workers and discuss their strengths and weaknesses.

🔧 **New language** Possessive adjectives
Aa Vocabulary Personality traits
🧩 **New skill** Describing your co-workers

 13.1 REWRITE THE SENTENCES, CORRECTING THE ERRORS

I run a team great, but Kezia be really lazy.
I run a great team, but Kezia is really lazy.

1 The new intern seems really bright and she is organized very.

_____

2 My manager doesn't ask employees nervous to give presentations.

_____

3 My director very bossy is and she is also hardworking.

_____

4 Sue and Robin are sometimes rudes to our clients.

_____

5 It's important to stay under pressure calm, even if you're very busy.

_____

6 Mushira is very intelligente, and she will bring a great deal to the team.

_____

7 It's impossible to feel relaxed when you work with people impatient.

_____

8 The people on my team are all very motivateds, and it's great to work with them.

_____

9 We are looking for a designer creative to join our busy production team.

_____

🔊

13.2 REWRITE THE SENTENCES, PUTTING THE WORDS IN THE CORRECT ORDER

is | calm. | Sarah | always

Sarah is always calm.

1 very | Ian | hardworking. | seems

_____

2 polite. | Kay | are | Jack | really | and

_____

3 is | Ben | bossy. | very

_____

4 always | Diane | dressed. | well | looks

_____

5 impatient. | really | is | Alex

_____

6 chef. | is | creative | a | Lenny

_____

7 is | great | This | team. | a

_____

8 very | Jo | organized. | seems

_____

9 bright. | very | seems | Harry

_____

13.3 LISTEN TO THE AUDIO AND MATCH THE PERSON IN EACH PICTURE WITH THE CORRECT ADJECTIVE

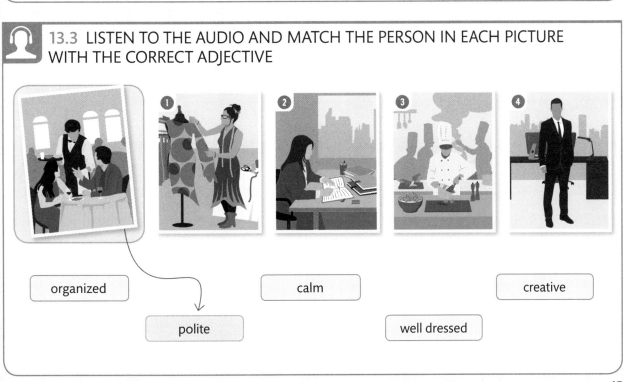

organized

calm

creative

polite

well dressed

13.4 FILL IN THE GAPS BY TURNING THE SUBJECT PRONOUNS INTO POSSESSIVE ADJECTIVES

James is very hardworking. _____*His*_____ (He) list of things to do is very long.

❶ _____ (We) team meetings are always interesting.

❷ Is this _____ (you) desk? It's very messy!

❸ _____ (I) team is very motivated.

❹ Is that _____ (they) design? It's great.

❺ Kevin is talking to _____ (he) manager.

❻ That's Tanya. _____ (She) phone manner is excellent.

❼ The company is very proud of _____ (it) reputation.

🔊

13.5 CROSS OUT THE INCORRECT WORD IN EACH SENTENCE

This laptop is ~~my~~ / mine.

❶ Is this he / his desk?

❷ We don't like theirs / their product.

❸ My / Mine manager is very smart.

❹ This report is your / yours.

❺ Jane does her / hers job well.

❻ They are proud of their / theirs reputation.

❼ Is this tablet her / hers?

❽ Their / Theirs manager is never late.

❾ Is this your / yours pen?

🔊

46

13.6 MARK THE SENTENCES THAT ARE CORRECT

Toms secretary will take the minutes. ☐
Tom's secretary will take the minutes. ☑

❶ The interns have just finished college. ☐
The intern's have just finished college. ☐

❷ Jorges reputation is well deserved. ☐
Jorge's reputation is well deserved. ☐

❸ Nuala's assistant is very helpful. ☐
Nualas assistant is very helpful. ☐

❹ Helens manager often works late. ☐
Helen's manager often works late. ☐

❺ Maria's co-workers are really friendly. ☐
Marias co-workers are really friendly. ☐

❻ The team members' are hardworking. ☐
The team members are hardworking. ☐

❼ Look at this ad. I like it's design. ☐
Look at this ad. I like its design. ☐

❽ Leroy's work is very impressive. ☐
Leroys' work is very impressive. ☐

❾ Are there any file's in the cabinet? ☐
Are there any files in the cabinet? ☐

❿ Johns confidence has grown this year. ☐
John's confidence has grown this year. ☐

⓫ Sams' presentation went really well. ☐
Sam's presentation went really well. ☐

⓬ The CEO's new assistant is very bright. ☐
The CEOs' new assistant is very bright. ☐

⓭ Their products are very popular. ☐
Their product's are very popular. ☐

⓮ That's my bosses parking space. ☐
That's my boss's parking space. ☐

⓯ Pablo's report is almost finished. ☐
Pablos report is almost finished. ☐

⓰ The company is pleased with it's new logo. ☐
The company is pleased with its new logo. ☐

⓱ Ethans' team is working on a new project. ☐
Ethan's team is working on a new project. ☐

◀))

13.7 USE THE CHART TO CREATE 14 CORRECT SENTENCES AND SAY THEM OUT LOUD

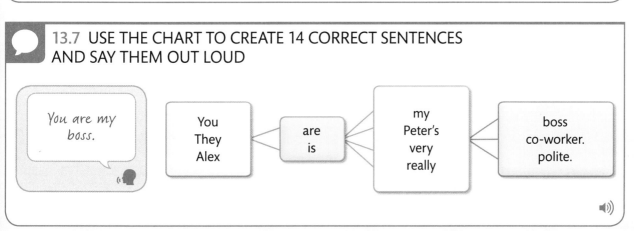

You are my boss.

| You / They / Alex | are / is | my / Peter's / very / really | boss / co-worker. / polite. |

◀))

47

14 Describing your job

One way of telling someone about your job is to use adjectives to describe it. Adjectives can also help you to make comparisons with other roles you have had.

🔧 **New language** Adjectives and comparatives
Aa Vocabulary Money and pay
🧩 **New skill** Describing your job to someone

 14.1 CROSS OUT THE INCORRECT WORD IN EACH SENTENCE

Sean has a very ~~interested~~ / interesting proposal.

1 Vihaan is very satisfied / satisfying with his office.

2 The new login system is rather annoyed / annoying.

3 The quarterly results are shocked / shocking.

4 The economic situation is quite worried / worrying.

5 We're excited / exciting about the new office.

6 Simone was tired / tiring after the course.

7 The profits were disappointed / disappointing.

8 John is confused / confusing about the schedule.

9 We were surprised / surprising by the results.

10 We thought the meeting was bored / boring.

11 I'm often exhausted / exhausting by Friday.

🔊

Aa 14.2 MATCH THE DEFINITIONS TO THE ADJECTIVES

| very tired | → | exhausted |

1 something that is not interesting — boring

2 unable to understand or think clearly — surprising

3 something that gives you enthusiasm — exhausted

4 something that is irritating — worried

5 something that is not expected — interesting

6 something you want to know more about — exciting

7 sad that something is not as good as expected — annoying

8 concerned or anxious about something — confused — disappointed

🔊

14.3 FILL IN THE GAPS USING THE ADJECTIVES FROM THE PANEL AND THEIR COMPARATIVE FORMS

Jan is ___excited___ about the news, but is ___more excited___ about her promotion.

❶ I am very _____ with the new project, but I'll be even _____ next week.

❷ Our new office is _____ , but the office in Beijing is _____ .

❸ My job is very _____ , but being unemployed is _____ .

❹ The meeting was _____ , but last week's was even _____ .

❺ John's flight ticket was _____ , but mine was _____ .

❻ Our new photocopier is _____ , but the HR department's is _____ .

❼ Claire's news was _____ , but Peter resigning was _____ .

❽ My current job is _____ , but my old one was _____ .

❾ The new furniture is _____ , but the furniture at G-Tech is _____ .

❿ This test is _____ , but the next one will be _____ .

⓫ My commute is _____ ; it's only 10 minutes. Pete's is even _____ .

comfortable	stressful	interesting	expensive	difficult	large
long	fast	~~excited~~	surprising	short	busy

49

14.4 REWRITE THE SENTENCES USING THE COMPARATIVE FORM OF THE ADJECTIVE IN BRACKETS

This contract is (good) than the old one.
This contract is better than the old one.

❶ Your printer is (quick) than ours.

❷ Today's meeting was (interesting) than usual.

❸ Growth was (bad) than we had expected.

❹ Sandra has been (successful) than last year.

❺ I'm feeling (good) after a week off work.

❻ There is (little) juice left than I thought.

❼ My new apartment is (close) to the center.

❽ The results are (good) than in the first quarter.

❾ We have an (early) start than usual today.

❿ Liam has taken a much (late) lunch break than everyone else.

⓫ This restaurant is (bad) than the others.

⓬ The flight was (expensive) than I expected.

14.5 MATCH THE BEGINNINGS OF THE SENTENCES TO THE CORRECT ENDINGS

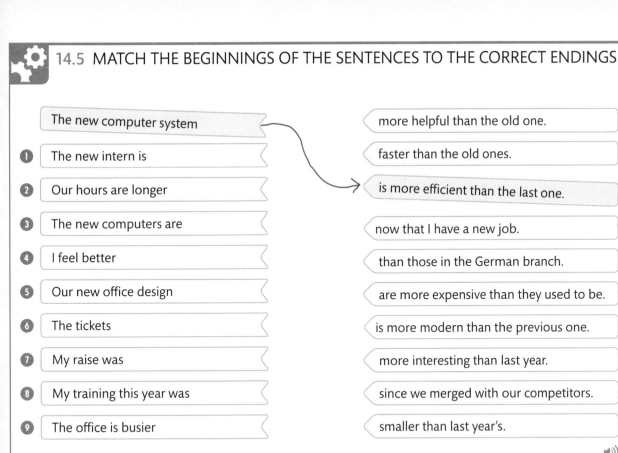

The new computer system — is more efficient than the last one.

1. The new intern is
2. Our hours are longer
3. The new computers are
4. I feel better
5. Our new office design
6. The tickets
7. My raise was
8. My training this year was
9. The office is busier

more helpful than the old one.

faster than the old ones.

is more efficient than the last one.

now that I have a new job.

than those in the German branch.

are more expensive than they used to be.

is more modern than the previous one.

more interesting than last year.

since we merged with our competitors.

smaller than last year's.

14.6 LISTEN TO THE AUDIO AND ANSWER THE QUESTIONS

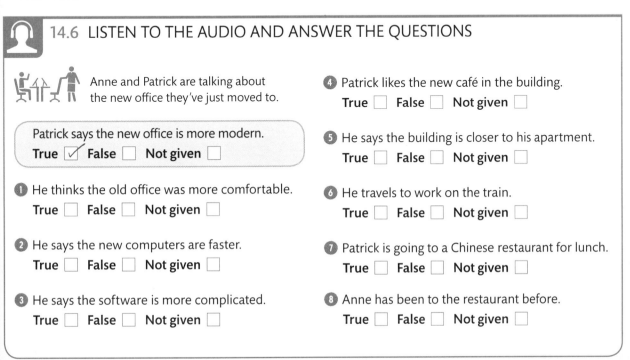

Anne and Patrick are talking about the new office they've just moved to.

Patrick says the new office is more modern.
True ✓ False ☐ Not given ☐

1. He thinks the old office was more comfortable.
True ☐ False ☐ Not given ☐

2. He says the new computers are faster.
True ☐ False ☐ Not given ☐

3. He says the software is more complicated.
True ☐ False ☐ Not given ☐

4. Patrick likes the new café in the building.
True ☐ False ☐ Not given ☐

5. He says the building is closer to his apartment.
True ☐ False ☐ Not given ☐

6. He travels to work on the train.
True ☐ False ☐ Not given ☐

7. Patrick is going to a Chinese restaurant for lunch.
True ☐ False ☐ Not given ☐

8. Anne has been to the restaurant before.
True ☐ False ☐ Not given ☐

15 Workplace routines

Employees have schedules, and workplaces also have their own routines and timetables. It is useful to be able to talk to colleagues about when things usually happen.

🔧 **New language** Prepositions of time
Aa Vocabulary Commuting and transportation
🧩 **New skill** Describing routines

15.1 REWRITE THE SENTENCES, PUTTING THE WORDS IN THE CORRECT ORDER

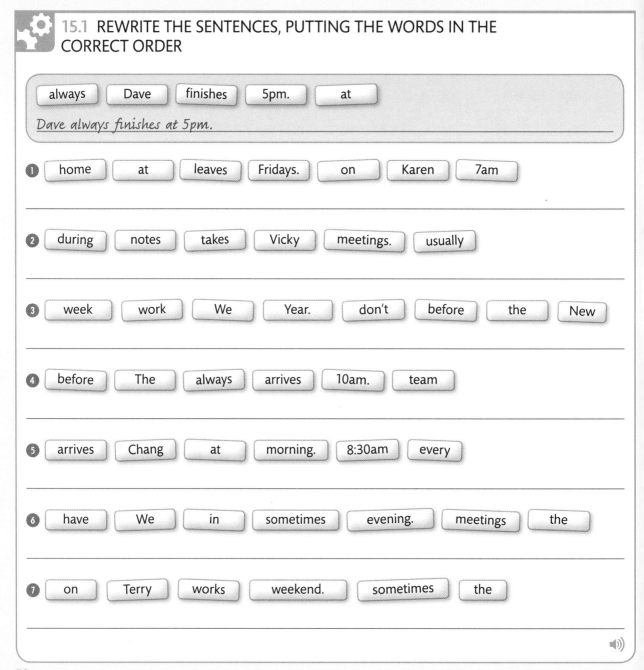

| always | Dave | finishes | 5pm. | at |

Dave always finishes at 5pm.

❶ | home | at | leaves | Fridays. | on | Karen | 7am |

_____

❷ | during | notes | takes | Vicky | meetings. | usually |

_____

❸ | week | work | We | Year. | don't | before | the | New |

_____

❹ | before | The | always | arrives | 10am. | team |

_____

❺ | arrives | Chang | at | morning. | 8:30am | every |

_____

❻ | have | We | in | sometimes | evening. | meetings | the |

_____

❼ | on | Terry | works | weekend. | sometimes | the |

_____

🔊

15.2 CROSS OUT THE INCORRECT WORD IN EACH SENTENCE, THEN SAY THE SENTENCES OUT LOUD

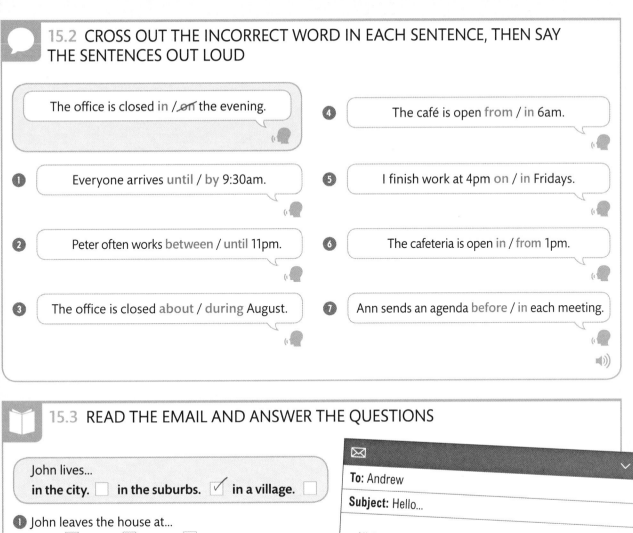

The office is closed in / ~~on~~ the evening.

4 The café is open from / in 6am.

1 Everyone arrives until / by 9:30am.

5 I finish work at 4pm on / in Fridays.

2 Peter often works between / until 11pm.

6 The cafeteria is open in / from 1pm.

3 The office is closed about / during August.

7 Ann sends an agenda before / in each meeting.

15.3 READ THE EMAIL AND ANSWER THE QUESTIONS

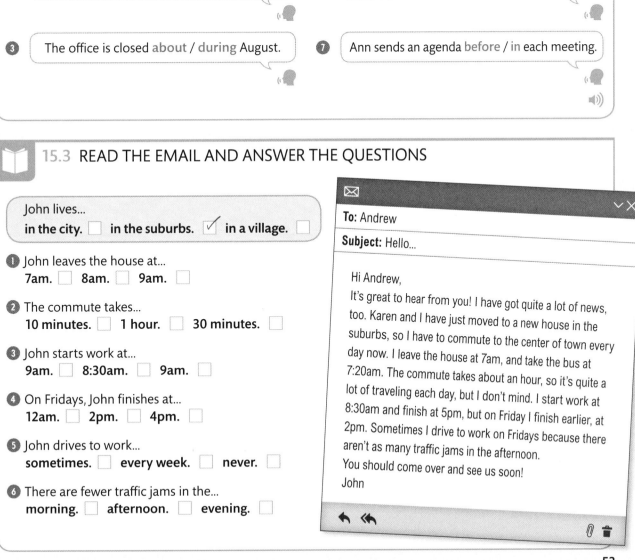

John lives...
in the city. ☐   in the suburbs. ☑   in a village. ☐

1 John leaves the house at...
7am. ☐   8am. ☐   9am. ☐

2 The commute takes...
10 minutes. ☐   1 hour. ☐   30 minutes. ☐

3 John starts work at...
9am. ☐   8:30am. ☐   9am. ☐

4 On Fridays, John finishes at...
12am. ☐   2pm. ☐   4pm. ☐

5 John drives to work...
sometimes. ☐   every week. ☐   never. ☐

6 There are fewer traffic jams in the...
morning. ☐   afternoon. ☐   evening. ☐

To: Andrew

Subject: Hello...

Hi Andrew,

It's great to hear from you! I have got quite a lot of news, too. Karen and I have just moved to a new house in the suburbs, so I have to commute to the center of town every day now. I leave the house at 7am, and take the bus at 7:20am. The commute takes about an hour, so it's quite a lot of traveling each day, but I don't mind. I start work at 8:30am and finish at 5pm, but on Friday I finish earlier, at 2pm. Sometimes I drive to work on Fridays because there aren't as many traffic jams in the afternoon.

You should come over and see us soon!

John

15.4 CROSS OUT THE INCORRECT WORD IN EACH SENTENCE

Sarah catches / ~~jumps~~ the bus near the park.

1 I drive because it's so comfortable / convenient.

2 Jim takes / drives the bus every morning.

3 Jack travels on / by bike when he can.

4 The rush / busy hour starts at 7am in my city.

5 Sam takes / makes the metro home each evening.

6 Raymond catches / drives his car to work.

7 I get on / in the bus near the museum.

8 I missed my connection / link.

9 Janet prefers to travel on / by train to work.

10 Karl takes / drives the bus home at night.

11 There are a lot of traffic blocks / jams in the city.

12 You should get off / from the tram at the library.

13 It's much cheaper to cycle / bike than drive.

14 I like to walk / walking to work in the summer.

15 I prefer to cycle / train to my office.

🔊

 15.5 MARK THE SENTENCES THAT ARE CORRECT

I leave my house before 6am. ✓
I leave my house in front of 6am. ☐

1 I car to work. ☐
I drive to work. ☐

2 We take the bus. ☐
We make the bus. ☐

3 Doug catches his bike to work. ☐
Doug rides his bike to work. ☐

4 I sometimes take a taxi home. ☐
I sometimes drive a taxi home. ☐

5 The buses run from 5am to 11pm. ☐
The buses run of 5am to 11pm. ☐

6 I go in train. ☐
I go by train. ☐

7 The train arrives on 5pm. ☐
The train arrives at 5pm. ☐

8 Sharon gets off the bus by the station. ☐
Sharon gets from the bus by the station. ☐

9 I like to go home from work on foot. ☐
I like to go home from work by foot. ☐

10 My train to work arrives on 7:45am. ☐
My train to work arrives at 7:45am. ☐

11 Traveling by train is comfortable. ☐
Traveling on train is comfortable. ☐

12 The train leaves at about 8pm. ☐
The train leaves at near 8pm. ☐

13 I travel on train every day. ☐
I travel by train every day. ☐

🔊

15.6 LISTEN TO THE AUDIO, THEN NUMBER THE PICTURES IN THE ORDER THEY ARE DESCRIBED

15.7 MATCH THE BEGINNINGS OF THE SENTENCES TO THE CORRECT ENDINGS

All the staff arrives ⟶ by 9:30am.

on the weekend.

1. There aren't many buses
2. Hank takes the bus because
3. The office stays open
4. I leave for work
5. Sally often walks to work
6. I take the train to work because
7. Ted takes notes
8. I always go to bed

until 10 in the evening.

during the summer.

it's cheaper than the train.

during meetings.

between 7 and 8am.

before 11pm.

it's faster than the bus.

16 Vocabulary

Aa 16.1 DAYS OF THE WEEK WRITE THE WORDS FROM THE PANEL UNDER THE CORRECT PICTURES

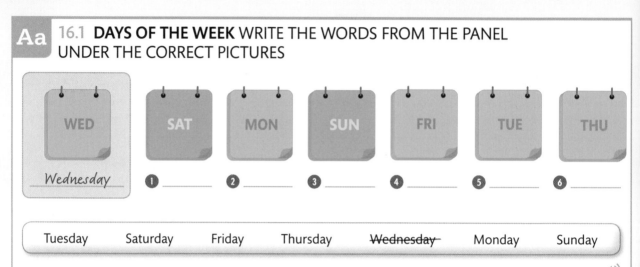

WED
Wednesday

SAT
❶ _____

MON
❷ _____

SUN
❸ _____

FRI
❹ _____

TUE
❺ _____

THU
❻ _____

| Tuesday | Saturday | Friday | Thursday | ~~Wednesday~~ | Monday | Sunday |

Aa 16.2 FREQUENCY PHRASES WRITE THE PHRASES FROM THE PANEL UNDER THE CORRECT PICTURES

quarterly

❶ _____

❷ _____

❸ _____

❹ _____

❺ _____

❻ _____

❼ _____

❽ _____

❾ _____

| hourly | ~~quarterly~~ | monthly | in the morning | before work |
| in the afternoon | in the evening | daily | three times a week | after work |

go running

1 _____

2 _____

3 _____

4 _____

5 _____

6 _____

7 _____

8 _____

9 _____

10 _____

11 _____

12 _____

13 _____

14 _____

15 _____

16 _____

17 _____

18 _____

19 _____

visit a museum / an art gallery   read   cook   meet friends   write   draw   watch a movie

go camping   take photos   see a play   go out for a meal   go cycling   play board games   do yoga

walk / hike   ~~go running~~   go shopping   stay (at) home   play sports   play an instrument

17 Hobbies and habits

When talking with colleagues about your hobbies and habits, you may want to use adverbs of frequency to say how often you do the activities.

⚙ **New language** Adverbs of frequency
Aa Vocabulary Hobbies and habits
🧩 **New skill** Talking about free time

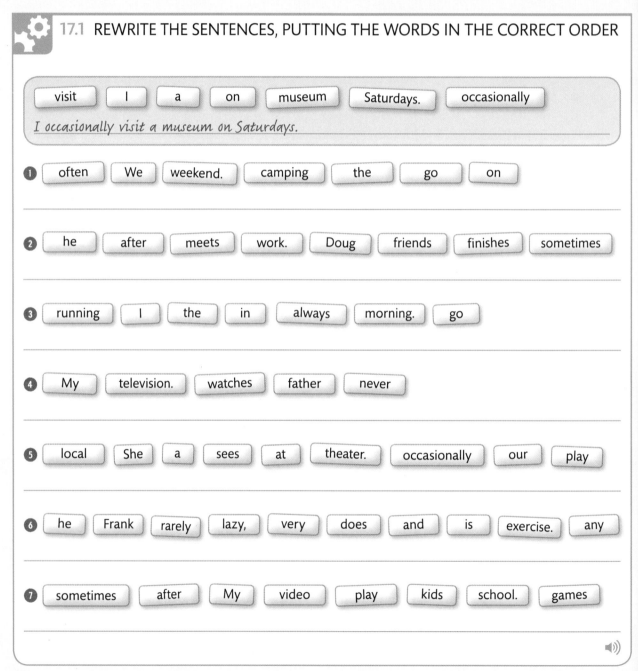

17.1 REWRITE THE SENTENCES, PUTTING THE WORDS IN THE CORRECT ORDER

| visit | I | a | on | museum | Saturdays. | occasionally |

I occasionally visit a museum on Saturdays.

1 | often | We | weekend. | camping | the | go | on |

2 | he | after | meets | work. | Doug | friends | finishes | sometimes |

3 | running | I | the | in | always | morning. | go |

4 | My | television. | watches | father | never |

5 | local | She | a | sees | at | theater. | occasionally | our | play |

6 | he | Frank | rarely | lazy, | very | does | and | is | exercise. | any |

7 | sometimes | after | My | video | play | kids | school. | games |

🔊

58

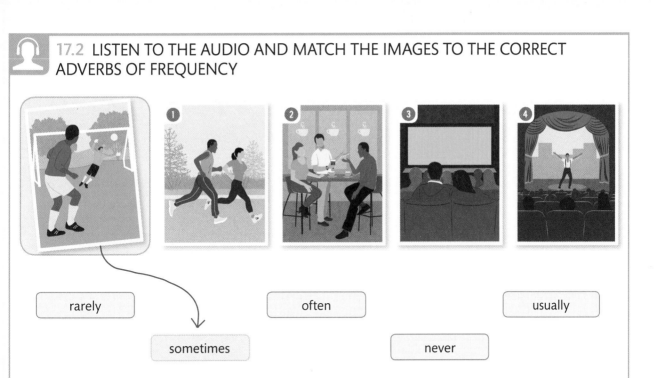

rarely

often

usually

sometimes

never

17.3 MATCH THE BEGINNINGS OF THE SENTENCES TO THE CORRECT ENDINGS

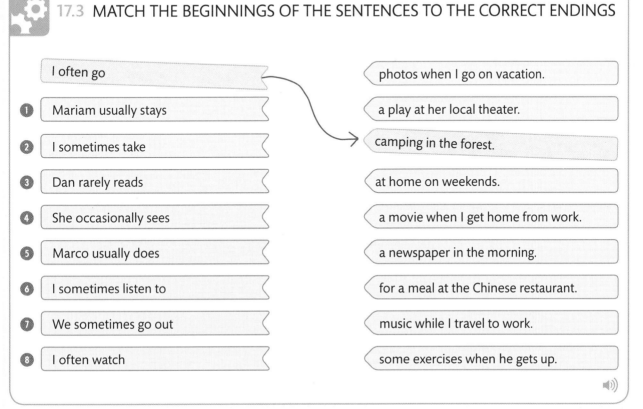

I often go

❶ Mariam usually stays

❷ I sometimes take

❸ Dan rarely reads

❹ She occasionally sees

❺ Marco usually does

❻ I sometimes listen to

❼ We sometimes go out

❽ I often watch

photos when I go on vacation.

a play at her local theater.

camping in the forest.

at home on weekends.

a movie when I get home from work.

a newspaper in the morning.

for a meal at the Chinese restaurant.

music while I travel to work.

some exercises when he gets up.

17.4 MARK THE SENTENCES THAT ARE CORRECT

This is the best way to get home. ✓
This is the most good way to get home. ☐

1 The earliest flight is at 9am. ☐
The most early flight is at 9am. ☐

2 Sydney is the most largest city in Australia. ☐
Sydney is the largest city in Australia. ☐

3 Dubai is the hottest place I've visited. ☐
Dubai is the most hottest place I've visited. ☐

4 This is the most expensive software we sell. ☐
This is the expensivest software we sell. ☐

5 The most far I've flown is to New Zealand. ☐
The farthest I've flown is to New Zealand. ☐

6 Spanish is the most easiest language to learn. ☐
Spanish is the easiest language to learn. ☐

7 Kraków is the most beautiful city in Poland. ☐
Kraków is the more beautiful city in Poland. ☐

8 The train is the most affordable way to travel. ☐
The train is the affordablest way to travel. ☐

9 This is the most interesting gallery in town. ☐
This is the most interestingest gallery in town. ☐

10 Hiroshi is most intelligent person I know. ☐
Hiroshi is the most intelligent person I know. ☐

11 That was the scariest film I've seen. ☐
That was the most scary film I've seen. ☐

🔊

17.5 SAY THE SENTENCES OUT LOUD, PUTTING THE ADJECTIVES INTO THEIR SUPERLATIVE FORMS

We had our ___worst___ (bad) results in 10 years.

1 The _____ (long) river in Brazil is the Amazon.

2 We'll have lunch at the _____ (close) café to the office.

3 I just watched the _____ (bad) presentation I've ever seen.

4 I think that snowboarding is the _____ (exciting) sport.

5 Sean lives the _____ (far) from the office.

6 Antonio is our _____ (loyal) employee.

7 This is the _____ (expensive) printer we have.

🔊

LEISURE WEEKLY

How do you spend your free time?

We speak to three different people about what they do in their time away from work.

Chloe Smith, 21

I get up early most days and usually do some exercises. I'm not very sporty, to be honest, but I go jogging twice a week. On the weekend I like to relax; I work in a bank, which is stressful. I go to the theater quite often and I sometimes do yoga on Saturday afternoons. I never watch sports. It's the most boring thing possible!

Pete McManus, 30

I like martial arts. I'm a member of a karate club, and I try to go there as regularly as possible. I think karate is the most exciting sport. It involves a lot of self-discipline. What else? Well, I occasionally go jogging. Oh, and I play tennis with my wife from time to time. You could say that I'm a sporty person!

Dan Stevens, 47

I'm not the most active person. I like to play video games with my friends in the evening. I sometimes watch soccer with my friends on weekends. There's a gym at my workplace, but I go there pretty rarely. My wife thinks I should get more exercise, but I hate working out. I'd much rather relax at home.

Who goes jogging twice a week?	Chloe ✓	Pete ☐	Dan ☐

1 Who rarely goes to the gym?   Chloe ☐   Pete ☐   Dan ☐

2 Who plays tennis with his wife?   Chloe ☐   Pete ☐   Dan ☐

3 Who is the most sporty?   Chloe ☐   Pete ☐   Dan ☐

4 Who thinks karate is the most exciting sport?   Chloe ☐   Pete ☐   Dan ☐

5 Who sometimes watches soccer?   Chloe ☐   Pete ☐   Dan ☐

6 Who does exercise early in the morning?   Chloe ☐   Pete ☐   Dan ☐

7 Who is a member of a sports club?   Chloe ☐   Pete ☐   Dan ☐

8 Who doesn't go jogging?   Chloe ☐   Pete ☐   Dan ☐

9 Who sometimes does yoga?   Chloe ☐   Pete ☐   Dan ☐

10 Who likes to play video games?   Chloe ☐   Pete ☐   Dan ☐

18 Past events

The past simple is often used when talking with co-workers about events that started and finished at a specific time in the recent or distant past.

⚙ New language The past simple
Aa Vocabulary Activities outside work
🧩 New skill Talking about past events

18.1 MARK THE SENTENCES THAT ARE CORRECT

Chris played soccer after work. ✓
Chris playd soccer after work. ☐

⑤ He went to the conference by car. ☐
He did went to the conference by car. ☐

① I didn't learn Spanish at school. ☐
I didn't learned Spanish at school. ☐

⑥ My manager not visited the factory. ☐
My manager didn't visit the factory. ☐

② We walking to the conference center. ☐
We walked to the conference center. ☐

⑦ Selma didn't walk to work today. ☐
Selma didn't walked to work today. ☐

③ John did lived in New York for 10 years. ☐
John lived in New York for 10 years. ☐

⑧ Jimish posted the report a week ago. ☐
Jimish post the report a week ago. ☐

④ Did the team discussed the merger? ☐
Did the team discuss the merger? ☐

⑨ Did Tom finish the report? ☐
Finished Tom the report? ☐

18.2 FILL IN THE GAPS BY PUTTING THE VERBS IN THE PAST SIMPLE

Jenny ___studied___ (study) hard, but she ___did not pass___ (not pass) the accounting exam.

① Akiko _____ (finish) her presentation, then she _____ (watch) some TV.

② I _____ (not watch) the game because I _____ (need) to prepare for the conference.

③ Derek _____ (want) to work somewhere interesting, so he _____ (move) to New York.

④ We _____ (arrive) late, but we _____ (not miss) the meeting.

⑤ Sally _____ (pass) her exams, and _____ (decide) to go to college.

18.3 REWRITE THE SENTENCES, PUTTING THE WORDS IN THE CORRECT ORDER

get | explain | Did | Peter | to | how | to | office? | the

Did Peter explain how to get to the office?

---

❶ the | Fred | me | conference | center. | showed | new

_____

❷ watched | about | We | documentary | an | Beijing. | interesting

_____

❸ company | started | years | at | about | this | ago. | Ramon | five

_____

❹ you | Did | presentation | enjoy | the | the | Indian economy? | about

_____

❺ play | It | yesterday, | rained | we | soccer. | so | didn't

_____

❻ cooked | Arnold | last | me | dinner | a | night. | delicious

_____

❼ about | Did | finish | Sam | report | the | product | new | range? | the

_____

❽ table | I | in | a | the | center. | in | restaurant | a | booked

_____

❾ the | Did Mike | tennis | on | with | CEO | new | Saturday? | play

_____

◀))

63

18.4 REWRITE THE SENTENCES AS QUESTIONS IN THE PAST SIMPLE

> Claire finished the presentation on Thursday.
> _Did Claire finish the presentation on Thursday?_

1 Paul started working for us more than five years ago.

_____

2 Sally explained how to use the new photocopier.

_____

3 It rained while they were in Indonesia.

_____

4 Clive picked up the guests from the railway station.

_____

5 Mark joined you for lunch at the Chinese restaurant.

_____

6 The team attended the conference in Paris last year.

_____

7 Philip played golf with the consultants last weekend.

_____

8 Carl and Marie walked to work again today.

_____

9 You watched the game yesterday.

_____

10 Janet showed you the new photocopier.

_____

11 Mo studied economics at Stanford University.

_____

12 The company invested $10 million in R&D.

_____

18.5 LISTEN TO THE AUDIO AND ANSWER THE QUESTIONS

Two co-workers are catching up after the weekend.

Ben visited York with his family.
True ✓ False ☐ Not given ☐

1 York is a very modern city.
True ☐ False ☐ Not given ☐

2 The family stayed in a hotel.
True ☐ False ☐ Not given ☐

3 The castle is over 1,000 years old.
True ☐ False ☐ Not given ☐

4 Helen visited a shopping mall.
True ☐ False ☐ Not given ☐

5 They visited the circus.
True ☐ False ☐ Not given ☐

6 In the evening they went to see a movie.
True ☐ False ☐ Not given ☐

7 Helen didn't enjoy the food in the restaurant.
True ☐ False ☐ Not given ☐

18.6 DESCRIBE WHAT EACH PERSON DID, SPEAKING OUT LOUD AND USING THE PAST SIMPLE FORM OF THE PHRASES IN THE PANEL

He played tennis.

walk to work   study for an exam   listen to the radio   ~~play tennis~~   travel to India   visit a friend

19 Dates and times

When making arrangements or talking about past or future events, it is important to talk about the time correctly. There are a number of ways to do this in English.

⚙ **New language** When things happen
Aa Vocabulary Telling the time
🧩 **New skill** Making appointments

19.1 LISTEN TO THE AUDIO AND MARK THE CORRECT TIMES

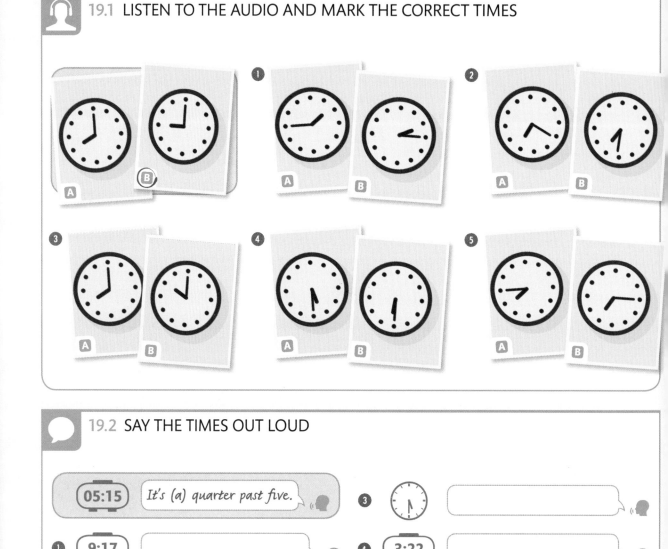

19.2 SAY THE TIMES OUT LOUD

05:15 · *It's (a) quarter past five.*

❶ **9:17**

❷

❸

❹ **3:22**

❺

19.3 REWRITE THE SENTENCES, PUTTING THE WORDS IN THE CORRECT ORDER

August | on | begins | conference | The | 4.

The conference begins on August 4.

① ends | June | tournament | 20. | soccer | The | on

_____

② Independence | on | American | is | 4th | Day | July. | the | of

_____

③ December | is | Christmas | on | 25. | Day

_____

④ September | on | birthday | My | is | 5. | wife's

_____

⑤ August | My | born | on | was | 3. | daughter

_____

🔊

19.4 LISTEN TO THE AUDIO AND ANSWER THE QUESTIONS

Rachel is talking about her life and the main events in it.

When was Rachel born?
1996 ☐ 1986 ✓ 1983 ☐

❶ What year did she move to New York?
2012 ☐ 2014 ☐ 2016 ☐

❷ When did she start working for her company?
August 2015 ☐ April 2015 ☐ April 2016 ☐

❸ When is her best friend's birthday?
January ☐ June ☐ July ☐

❹ Where does her best friend come from?
Scotland ☐ Switzerland ☐ Sweden ☐

❺ When is Rachel's wedding anniversary?
May 1 ☐ May 3 ☐ May 4 ☐

20 Career history

When you meet new co-workers or attend an interview, people may ask about your previous jobs. It is important to use correct verb forms when talking about the past.

⚙ **New language** Past simple irregular verbs
Aa Vocabulary Jobs and workplaces
🧩 **New skill** Talking about previous jobs

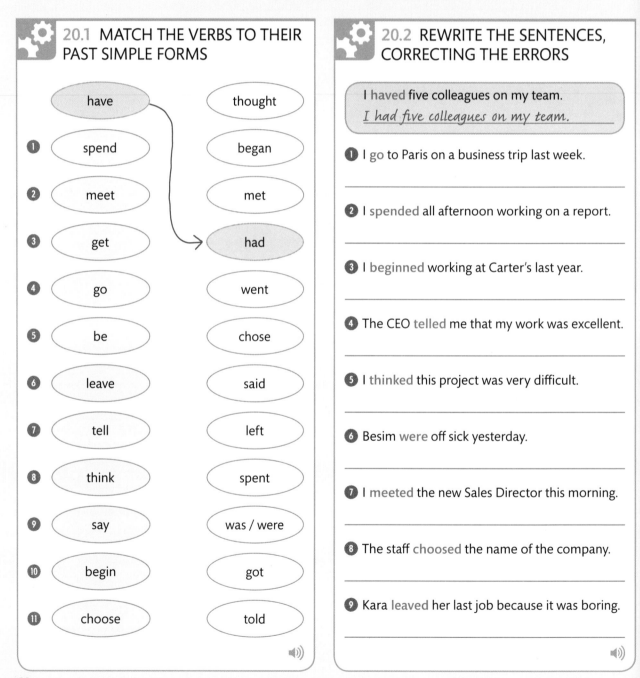

20.1 MATCH THE VERBS TO THEIR PAST SIMPLE FORMS

have → had

thought

1 spend — began

2 meet — met

3 get → had

4 go — went

5 be — chose

6 leave — said

7 tell — left

8 think — spent

9 say — was / were

10 begin — got

11 choose — told

20.2 REWRITE THE SENTENCES, CORRECTING THE ERRORS

I **haved** five colleagues on my team.
I had five colleagues on my team.

1 I **go** to Paris on a business trip last week.
_____

2 I **spended** all afternoon working on a report.
_____

3 I **beginned** working at Carter's last year.
_____

4 The CEO **telled** me that my work was excellent.
_____

5 I **thinked** this project was very difficult.
_____

6 Besim **were** off sick yesterday.
_____

7 I **meeted** the new Sales Director this morning.
_____

8 The staff **choosed** the name of the company.
_____

9 Kara **leaved** her last job because it was boring.
_____

20.3 FILL IN THE GAPS BY PUTTING THE VERBS IN THE PAST SIMPLE

My first job _____was_____ (be) in a supermarket.

❶ I _____ (meet) the International Marketing Director last week.

❷ I _____ (have) a demanding boss.

❸ I _____ (leave) my last job because it was badly paid.

❹ I _____ (get) to work very early today.

❺ They _____ (go) to the New York office last month.

❻ The staff _____ (choose) new chairs for the office.

❼ Sally _____ (think) that Rohit's presentation went well.

20.4 MATCH THE QUESTIONS TO THE CORRECT ANSWERS

How many people were on your team? → There were five of us.

❶ When did you start working at the café?

❷ Where did you work on your first job?

❸ What did you do as a nanny?

❹ Who did you meet as a journalist?

❺ How did you get your job as a director?

❻ What did you wear on your last job?

I met many interesting people.

There were five of us.

We had a black and white uniform.

I took the children to school.

I started work there after I left school.

I worked in a bank at the start of my career.

I worked hard and studied for an MBA.

20.5 LISTEN TO THE AUDIO, THEN NUMBER THE PICTURES IN THE ORDER THEY ARE DESCRIBED

A

B 1

C

D

E

F

G

H

20.6 CROSS OUT THE INCORRECT WORD IN EACH SENTENCE, THEN SAY THE SENTENCES OUT LOUD

We had / ~~haved~~ a very demanding boss in the marketing department.

1. I feeled / felt very well respected by my team leader.

2. The Head of Sales taught / teached me to give interesting presentations.

3. My brother made / maked a delicious cake, which I took to work for my birthday.

4. The staff choosed / chose the pictures for the meeting rooms, and they look great.

5. I left / leaved my last job because I didn't get along with the customers.

6. I spended / spent all of yesterday writing a sales report and now I'm very tired.

21 Company history

The past simple can be used to describe repeated or single actions in a company's history. These actions can last for a short or long time.

🔧 **New language** Past simple with time markers
Aa Vocabulary Describing trends
🧩 **New skill** Describing a company's history

🔧 **21.1 FILL IN THE GAPS USING THE WORDS IN THE PANEL**

I _____*founded*_____ Bee Designs in 2010.

1 We _____ a new range of apps last year.

2 At _____ , we only had four employees.

3 Two years _____ , we opened our tenth store.

4 The company _____ with a competitor a year ago.

5 A new Director of Marketing _____ working here last year.

| started |
| ago |
| merged |
| launched |
| ~~founded~~ |
| first |

🔊

🔧 **21.2 REWRITE THE SENTENCES, CORRECTING THE ERRORS**

Maria Hill opened the first Hill Shoe Store past 2015.
Maria Hill opened the first Hill Shoe Store in 2015.

1 At the first, we only had one store.

_____

2 We open a new flagship store last month.

_____

3 We launch an exciting new app last year.

_____

4 A new Director of HR started working here six months before.

_____

🔊

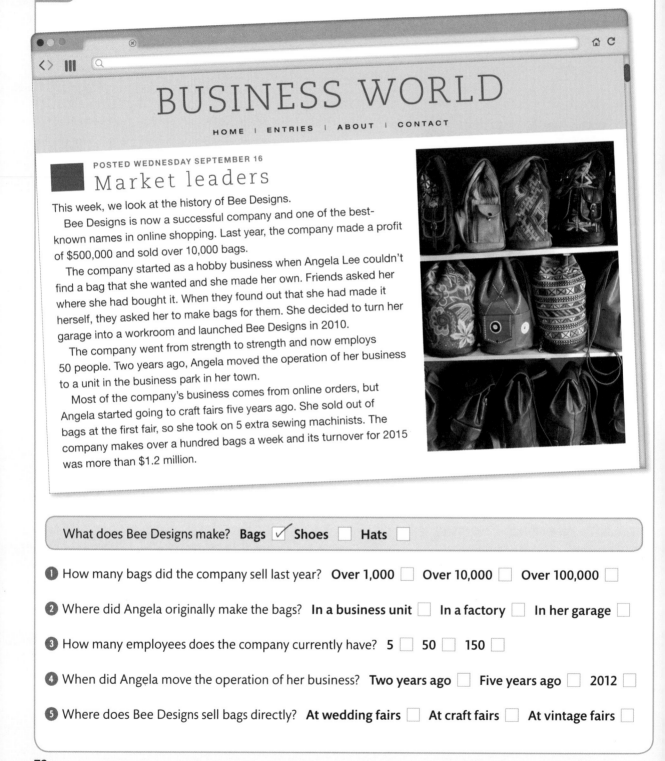

BUSINESS WORLD

HOME | ENTRIES | ABOUT | CONTACT

POSTED WEDNESDAY SEPTEMBER 16

Market leaders

This week, we look at the history of Bee Designs.

Bee Designs is now a successful company and one of the best-known names in online shopping. Last year, the company made a profit of $500,000 and sold over 10,000 bags.

The company started as a hobby business when Angela Lee couldn't find a bag that she wanted and she made her own. Friends asked her where she had bought it. When they found out that she had made it herself, they asked her to make bags for them. She decided to turn her garage into a workroom and launched Bee Designs in 2010.

The company went from strength to strength and now employs 50 people. Two years ago, Angela moved the operation of her business to a unit in the business park in her town.

Most of the company's business comes from online orders, but Angela started going to craft fairs five years ago. She sold out of bags at the first fair, so she took on 5 extra sewing machinists. The company makes over a hundred bags a week and its turnover for 2015 was more than $1.2 million.

What does Bee Designs make? **Bags** ☑ **Shoes** ☐ **Hats** ☐

① How many bags did the company sell last year? **Over 1,000** ☐ **Over 10,000** ☐ **Over 100,000** ☐

② Where did Angela originally make the bags? **In a business unit** ☐ **In a factory** ☐ **In her garage** ☐

③ How many employees does the company currently have? **5** ☐ **50** ☐ **150** ☐

④ When did Angela move the operation of her business? **Two years ago** ☐ **Five years ago** ☐ **2012** ☐

⑤ Where does Bee Designs sell bags directly? **At wedding fairs** ☐ **At craft fairs** ☐ **At vintage fairs** ☐

21.4 LISTEN TO THE AUDIO AND MATCH THE IMAGES TO THE CORRECT TIME MARKERS

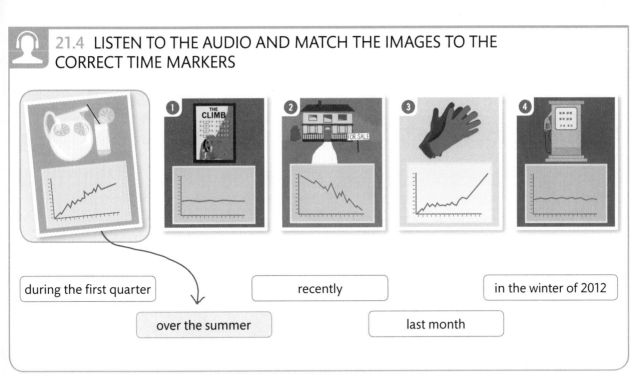

during the first quarter

recently

in the winter of 2012

over the summer

last month

21.5 CROSS OUT THE INCORRECT WORDS IN EACH SENTENCE, THEN SAY THE SENTENCES OUT LOUD

The number of sales decreased / decrease, but profits go / went up.

1 Recent / Last spring, sales of umbrellas rising / rose because it was wet.

2 UK sales rose up / went up in 2011, but falled / fell in 2012.

3 At / In first, the value of shares in the company remain / remained steady.

4 Online marketing costs increasing / increased and sales also rose / rised.

22 Vocabulary

Aa 22.1 MAKING ARRANGEMENTS WRITE THE PHRASES FROM THE PANEL UNDER THE CORRECT PICTURES

to book a meeting room

1 _____

2 _____

3 _____

8 _____

9 _____

10 _____

11 _____

16 _____

17 _____

18 _____

19 _____

Aa 22.2 ACCEPTING AND DECLINING WRITE THE PHRASES FROM THE PANEL UNDER THE CORRECT DEFINITIONS

To be convenient

to suit someone

1 To occur unexpectedly

_____

4 Cannot go to

_____

5 To be pleased about something that is going to happen

_____

74

4 _____

5 _____

6 _____

7 _____

12 _____

13 _____

14 _____

15 _____

to miss a meeting   refreshments   café   to invite someone   agenda   restaurant
to attend a meeting   evening   ~~to book a meeting room~~   morning   calendar
to decline an invitation   appointment   running late   reception   boardroom
conference room   to accept an invitation   afternoon   office

🔊

---

2 To decide that a planned event will not happen

_____

3 To have lots to do

_____

6 To decide on a new time and date for a meeting

_____

to cancel   ~~to suit someone~~   to come up
to reschedule   to look forward to
to be busy   to be unable to attend

🔊

23 Talking about your plans

One way of making plans with a co-worker or client is by using the present continuous to talk about what you are doing at the moment, or plans in the future.

⚙ **New language** The present continuous
Aa Vocabulary Making arrangements
🧩 **New skill** Talking about your plans

 23.1 FILL IN THE GAPS BY PUTTING THE VERBS IN THE PRESENT CONTINUOUS

> Steve ___is working___ (work) from home today. He ___is writing___ (write) the report.

1 The company _____ (lose) money, so we _____ (plan) a restructure.

2 Stacy _____ (not work) in the office today. She _____ (visit) the factory.

3 Dan _____ (meet) a new client. They _____ (chat) in the meeting room.

4 Colin _____ (start) a new project. He _____ (work) with Angela.

5 The head office _____ (relocate) to Delhi. We _____ (move) this week.

6 Profits _____ (fall) this year, and the team _____ (feel) nervous.

7 Anika _____ (work) late tonight. She _____ (prepare) a presentation.

8 Sue and Clive _____ (have) lunch downtown. They _____ (eat) Chinese.

9 I _____ (go) on vacation next week. I _____ (miss) the training day.

10 Our company _____ (sell) a lot to India. We _____ (open) an office in Mumbai.

11 Our secretary _____ (retire). We _____ (recruit) a new one.

12 Sam and Sue are _____ (discuss) the report. They _____ (plan) a meeting about it.

13 Chrissie _____ (choose) a new team. She _____ (consider) Paul for a position.

14 Alex _____ (leave) the company. He _____ (move) to New York.

◀))

23.2 REWRITE THE SENTENCES, PUTTING THE WORDS IN THE CORRECT ORDER

Doug   reading?   What   is

What is Doug reading?

4 the   Are   you   agenda?   printing

_____

1 are   Who   meeting?   you

_____

5 company   the   moving?   Is

_____

2 writing   the   Tim   report?   Is

_____

6 you   When   retiring?   are

_____

3 today?   Are   presenting   Kim and Jo

_____

7 you   are   promoting?   Who

_____

23.3 REWRITE THE STATEMENTS AS QUESTIONS IN THE PRESENT CONTINUOUS

Tom is translating the new contract today.
Is Tom translating the new contract today?

1 The conference is taking place in Venice next April.

_____

2 Leanne is giving a presentation on the takeover plans.

_____

3 Our owners are hoping to buy our biggest competitor.

_____

4 Brendan is programming the software for new machinery.

_____

5 We're taking time off in August this year.

_____

23.4 MARK THE SENTENCES THAT ARE CORRECT

Where are you working on Friday? ☑
Where does you work on Friday? ☐

1 Are you have lunch at 1pm today? ☐
Are you having lunch at 1pm today? ☐

2 Tom will going to the conference today. ☐
Tom is going to the conference today. ☐

3 Is John working until 7pm again? ☐
Does John working until 7pm again? ☐

4 We are traveling to New York again. ☐
We are travel to New York again. ☐

5 Is you coming to the meeting on Friday? ☐
Are you coming to the meeting on Friday? ☐

6 Will you visiting the factory next month? ☐
Are you visiting the factory next month? ☐

7 I'm not taking time off in August. ☐
I amn't taking time off in August. ☐

8 The head office will moving in the spring. ☐
The head office is moving in the spring. ☐

9 Fran aren't coming to the office tomorrow. ☐
Fran isn't coming to the office tomorrow. ☐

10 What are you doing on Tuesday? ☐
What you are doing on Tuesday? ☐

11 Sam be meeting the client this afternoon. ☐
Sam is meeting the client this afternoon. ☐

12 Tim is leaving work at 5pm today. ☐
Tim leaving work at 5pm today. ☐

🔊

23.5 LISTEN TO THE AUDIO AND ANSWER THE QUESTIONS

Clare is calling her colleague, Frank, to arrange a meeting with him.

Clare needs to arrange a meeting about...
the new sales strategy. ☑
the new recruits. ☐
the health and safety presentation. ☐

1 On Monday morning, Frank is...
attending a course. ☐
going to the dentist. ☐
visiting the factory. ☐

2 On Monday afternoon, Clare is...
free. ☐
attending a course. ☐
giving a presentation. ☐

3 On Tuesday, Frank is...
celebrating his birthday. ☐
celebrating his wedding anniversary. ☐
going on vacation. ☐

4 In the evening, he is...
going to a film. ☐
going to a restaurant. ☐
going to the theater. ☐

5 On Thursday at 2pm, Clare is...
meeting Pete. ☐
having lunch. ☐
visiting the factory. ☐

6 They are both available at...
2:30pm on Thursday. ☐
3:30pm on Thursday. ☐
2:30pm on Friday. ☐

23.6 READ THE SCHEDULE, THEN RESPOND TO THE AUDIO, SPEAKING OUT LOUD

July

Monday	Tuesday	Wednesday	Thursday	Friday
10am Give presentation to the interns		12 noon Flight to Edinburgh departs	11:30am Return to London	
2pm Have lunch with the IT team				
	3pm Meet the new clients from Germany		3pm Give report to CEO	
				7pm Sandra's leaving party

What are you doing on Monday morning?

I'm giving a presentation to the interns at 10am.

3 Where are you going on Wednesday?

1 Where are you going on Monday afternoon?

4 What time are you returning on Thursday?

2 What time are you meeting the clients?

5 Where are you going on Friday evening?

English speakers often use set phrases to signal that they want to interrupt without being rude. There are a number of ways to communicate your opinion politely.

⚙ New language Interruptions and opinions
Aa Vocabulary Environmental issues
🧩 New skill Giving opinions politely

24.1 MARK WHETHER EACH INTERRUPTION IS POLITE OR IMPOLITE

I'm sorry, but I can't agree with you there.
Polite ✓   **Impolite** ☐

1 Excuse me, but I agree with Stacey here.
Polite ☐   **Impolite** ☐

2 What are you talking about? That's wrong.
Polite ☐   **Impolite** ☐

3 I'm afraid I have to disagree with you about that.
Polite ☐   **Impolite** ☐

4 Could I just say that there are other options.
Polite ☐   **Impolite** ☐

5 Sorry to interrupt, but I have different figures.
Polite ☐   **Impolite** ☐

6 That's absolute nonsense.
Polite ☐   **Impolite** ☐

7 If I could just come in here, Robert.
Polite ☐   **Impolite** ☐

🔊

24.2 LISTEN TO THE AUDIO AND ANSWER THE QUESTIONS

Dan and Susan are talking at a meeting.

The meeting is about a new policy.
True ✓   **False** ☐   **Not given** ☐

1 Susan wants the company to develop new vehicles.
True ☐   **False** ☐   **Not given** ☐

2 Dan agrees with Susan's suggestion.
True ☐   **False** ☐   **Not given** ☐

3 The company leaves a bad carbon footprint.
True ☐   **False** ☐   **Not given** ☐

4 Dan thinks the workers should use the metro.
True ☐   **False** ☐   **Not given** ☐

5 Agrocorp are developing a motorcycle.
True ☐   **False** ☐   **Not given** ☐

6 The company will develop electric vehicles soon.
True ☐   **False** ☐   **Not given** ☐

7 Agrocorp employees recycle at home.
True ☐   **False** ☐   **Not given** ☐

24.3 RESPOND OUT LOUD TO THE AUDIO, FILLING IN THE GAPS USING THE WORDS IN THE PANEL

This will lead to a fall in profits.

Sorry to _____*disagree*_____ , but my figures are different.

1 The company might lose millions of dollars.

I'm sorry. I'm not sure I _____ .

2 These clothes won't appeal to people in China.

Sorry, but in my _____ they will sell well.

3 We need to increase our focus on the youth market.

I can see your _____ , but I still think senior citizens are more important.

4 We had exactly the same problem last year.

If I could just _____ in here and mention the good news from France.

5 The figures show a dramatic fall this year.

_____ me, but my figures tell a different story.

6 We need to employ two new team members.

_____ I just say...? The budget won't cover it.

7 India will be our biggest market in 2050.

I'm not _____ I agree. Sales to China are growing faster.

8 And if we sell our new software...

Sorry to _____ , but the software is not ready yet.

| come | interrupt | agree | excuse | point | ~~disagree~~ | could | sure | opinion |

24.4 CROSS OUT THE INCORRECT WORD IN EACH SENTENCE

Claire's ~~timed~~ / scheduled a meeting for later. She'll send the agenda to everyone soon.

1 I'm afraid Sean can't make it to the meeting and has given / sent his apologies.

2 Shall we take / make a vote on the new strategy to see what course of action to take?

3 Ramona will take / recall the minutes and email them to everyone after the meeting.

4 I agree with the motion. How about / for you? What do you think about it?

5 If I could just disturb / interrupt for a moment. I think we need to take a vote on this.

6 That sums up most of the issues we are facing. I just have a few finishing / closing remarks.

7 Claude is the chair, so he has the casting / choosing vote if there is a tie.

8 The chair / seat of our budget meetings likes to keep his closing remarks very short.

9 I read through / up the agenda before the meeting, so I know what we will be talking about.

Aa 24.5 MATCH THE DEFINITIONS TO THE WORDS

make something usable again	footprint
1 the mark or effect something leaves behind	reuse
2 environmentally friendly	recycle
3 to use something again	green
4 natural products you can use	environment
5 things we do not need or want	reduce
6 the natural world around us	resources
7 make an amount smaller	waste

25 Agreeing and disagreeing

When you react to someone's opinion, it is important to be polite and respectful. This is especially important when you disagree with someone.

🔧 **New language** Reacting to opinions
Aa Vocabulary Agreeing and disagreeing
🧩 **New skill** Discussing opinions

25.1 MARK THE BEST REPLY TO EACH STATEMENT

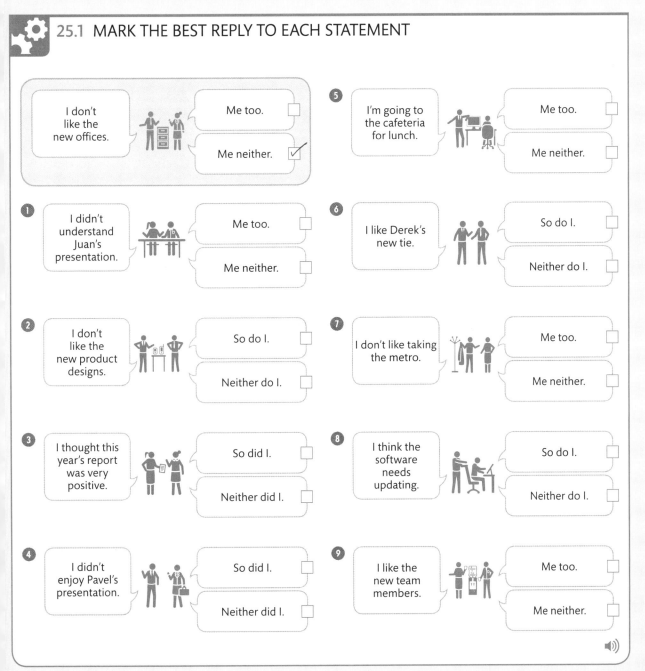

I don't like the new offices.
- Me too. ☐
- Me neither. ☑

1 I didn't understand Juan's presentation.
- Me too. ☐
- Me neither. ☐

2 I don't like the new product designs.
- So do I. ☐
- Neither do I. ☐

3 I thought this year's report was very positive.
- So did I. ☐
- Neither did I. ☐

4 I didn't enjoy Pavel's presentation.
- So did I. ☐
- Neither did I. ☐

5 I'm going to the cafeteria for lunch.
- Me too. ☐
- Me neither. ☐

6 I like Derek's new tie.
- So do I. ☐
- Neither do I. ☐

7 I don't like taking the metro.
- Me too. ☐
- Me neither. ☐

8 I think the software needs updating.
- So do I. ☐
- Neither do I. ☐

9 I like the new team members.
- Me too. ☐
- Me neither. ☐

🔊

Aa 25.2 MATCH THE STATEMENTS TO THE RESPONSES

I think the new interns are great.	So did I. He's so entertaining.
1 We should buy a new photocopier.	I'll ask the secretary to send it again.
2 I loved Pablo's presentation.	Me too. They are really helpful.
3 We need to invest more in training.	I suppose so. It will be expensive though.
4 I didn't receive the agenda.	Exactly. I didn't understand it at all.
5 I don't like the cafeteria much.	I agree. The team could improve their skills.
6 I like the new office furniture.	Absolutely. We should promote her.
7 The presentation was really confusing.	I agree. I learned some new skills.
8 The training was useful.	Me neither. The food's very bland.
9 The new HR assistant is really hard working.	So do I. It's very comfortable.

◀))

25.3 FILL IN THE GAPS USING THE WORDS IN THE PANEL

I'm sorry, but we disagree ____with____ the price.

1 I'm _____ we'll have to cancel the meeting.

2 I'm sorry, but I _____ with you.

3 I _____ disagree with you about this.

4 I'm really not _____ about that design.

5 I'm _____ , Pete, but I don't agree with you.

6 I don't agree at _____ . It won't work.

7 I'm not _____ about this. Can we talk later?

8 I'm afraid I _____ agree with you at all.

9 I don't _____ at all with the merger.

10 You _____ be right, but I'm not sure.

11 Sorry, but I disagree _____ this plan.

with	totally	afraid	sorry	don't	sure
could	all	disagree	sure	agree	~~with~~

◀))

84

25.4 LISTEN TO THE AUDIO AND ANSWER THE QUESTIONS

Two colleagues, Jenny and Greg, are discussing applicants for a job.

How does Jenny feel about the candidates?

She likes all of them. ✓

She likes some of them. ☐

She dislikes all of them. ☐

❶ Jenny thinks it's going to be an easy choice.

Greg strongly agrees with her. ☐

Greg agrees with her. ☐

Greg disagrees with her. ☐

❷ Jenny thinks John is a strong candidate.

Greg thinks he has lots of enthusiasm. ☐

Greg thinks he doesn't have enough experience. ☐

Greg thinks he has enough qualifications. ☐

❸ Greg thinks they need someone with experience.

Jenny strongly agrees. ☐

Jenny disagrees. ☐

Jenny strongly disagrees. ☐

❹ Jenny thinks Paula could be a good candidate.

Greg agrees. ☐

Greg strongly agrees. ☐

Greg disagrees. ☐

❺ Greg suggests they send Paula on a course.

Jenny agrees. ☐

Jenny strongly agrees. ☐

Jenny strongly disagrees. ☐

25.5 CROSS OUT THE INCORRECT WORD IN EACH SENTENCE, THEN SAY THE SENTENCES OUT LOUD

I agree / ~~argue~~ with you about the new IT system.

❶ We totally / perfectly agree about the redesign.

❷ I can't agree with you in / at all about the downsizing.

❸ We're frightened / afraid we totally disagree.

❹ You could / would be right, but I need more evidence.

❺ I'm not sure about / with the latest business plan.

26 Health and safety

Many workplaces issue guidelines for how to avoid accidents and stay safe. In English, this topic often uses specialist vocabulary and reflexive pronouns.

⚙ **New language** Reflexive pronouns
Aa Vocabulary Health and safety at work
🧩 **New skill** Talking about safety at work

26.1 MARK THE SENTENCES THAT ARE CORRECT

Anita signed herself up for the course. ☑
Anita signed itself up for the course. ☐

④ Jan cut herself on the machinery. ☐
She cut itself on the machinery. ☐

① Roger hurt him when he slipped. ☐
Roger hurt himself when he slipped. ☐

⑤ We enjoyed ourselves at the office party. ☐
We enjoyed ourself at the office party. ☐

② She burned herself on the coffee maker. ☐
She burned himself on the coffee maker. ☐

⑥ Juan cut yourself in the kitchen. ☐
Juan cut himself in the kitchen. ☐

③ Ron blames itself for the accident. ☐
Ron blames himself for the accident. ☐

⑦ We need to protect himself from risks. ☐
We need to protect ourselves from risks. ☐

🔊

26.2 CROSS OUT THE INCORRECT WORD IN EACH SENTENCE, THEN SAY THE SENTENCES OUT LOUD

We locked ourselves / ~~themselves~~ in the factory last week. 🗣

① I hurt yourself / myself when I moved the photocopier. 🗣

② They should prepare themselves / themself for the course. 🗣

③ Claire's cut herself / itself on the equipment. 🗣

④ Have you all signed yourself / yourselves up for the course? 🗣

⑤ Sam is teaching himself / hisself Japanese. 🗣

🔊

26.3 READ THE ARTICLE AND ANSWER THE QUESTIONS

Many employees are afraid of a fire in their building.
True ☑ **False** ☐ **Not given** ☐

❶ You should leave the building as quickly as possible.
True ☐ **False** ☐ **Not given** ☐

❷ You should turn off electrical appliances.
True ☐ **False** ☐ **Not given** ☐

❸ If you smell a fire, activate the fire alarm.
True ☐ **False** ☐ **Not given** ☐

❹ If you find a large fire, use an extinguisher to fight the fire.
True ☐ **False** ☐ **Not given** ☐

❺ You should take care to close doors behind you.
True ☐ **False** ☐ **Not given** ☐

❻ You should make sure you take your belongings with you.
True ☐ **False** ☐ **Not given** ☐

❼ You should go to the assembly point and wait.
True ☐ **False** ☐ **Not given** ☐

❽ You can go back to your office when the alarm stops.
True ☐ **False** ☐ **Not given** ☐

DAILY NEWS

A Burning Issue
What to do when you hear the fire alarm

A fire in the workplace is what 63% of employees fear the most. But there are some simple steps that you can follow to make sure you stay safe. First of all, don't panic: remember the instructions from your fire drill. If you smell smoke, activate the fire alarm. You should only use a fire extinguisher on a small fire. You should stay calm and leave the building using the stairs. Don't use the elevator, even if you are not fit. You should also leave all your belongings at your desk—don't waste time. Then, go to the nearest assembly point and stay there (even if the alarm has stopped) until the fire officer tells you it is safe to return.

Fire extinguisher

26.4 FILL IN THE GAPS USING THE WORDS IN THE PANEL

If you discover a fire, set off the _fire alarm_ .

❸ Medical equipment is kept in the _____.

❶ An _____ is used to stop small fires.

❹ Each fire _____ has a sign above the door.

❷ If you hear the fire alarm, go to the _____.

❺ You practice leaving the building during a _____.

| fire drill | extinguisher | escape | ~~fire alarm~~ | first aid kit | assembly area |

🔊

87

Suggestions and advice

When there are everyday problems in the workplace, it is useful to know how to make suggestions and offer advice. There are several ways to do this in English.

⚙ **New language** Prefixes and suffixes
Aa **Vocabulary** Everyday workplace problems
🧩 **New skill** Making suggestions

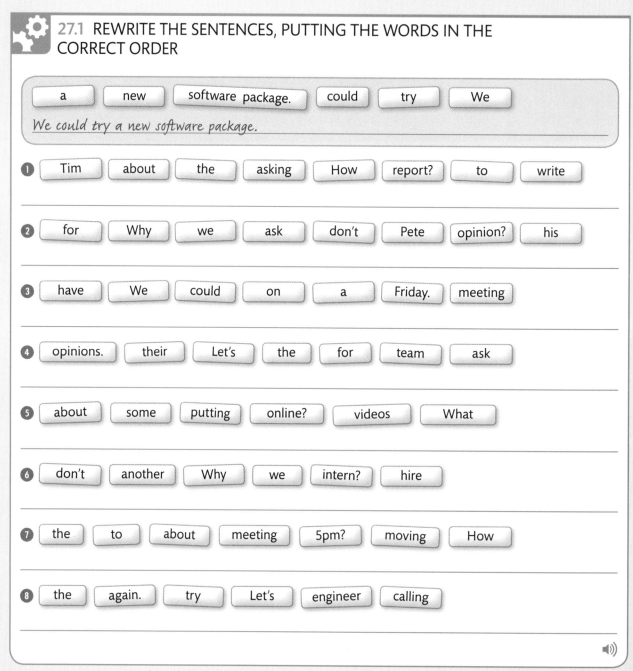

27.1 REWRITE THE SENTENCES, PUTTING THE WORDS IN THE CORRECT ORDER

| a | new | software package. | could | try | We |

We could try a new software package.

1 | Tim | about | the | asking | How | report? | to | write |

2 | for | Why | we | ask | don't | Pete | opinion? | his |

3 | have | We | could | on | a | Friday. | meeting |

4 | opinions. | their | Let's | the | for | team | ask |

5 | about | some | putting | online? | videos | What |

6 | don't | another | Why | we | intern? | hire |

7 | the | to | about | meeting | 5pm? | moving | How |

8 | the | again. | try | Let's | engineer | calling |

🔊

88

27.2 MATCH THE WORKPLACE PROBLEMS TO THE SUGGESTIONS AND ADVICE

I've been at my desk all day.	She should go home and rest.
1 Sally doesn't feel well.	You should go on a training course.
2 I've lost my copy of the agenda.	You should go for a walk.
3 I don't understand the new program.	You should order some more.
4 There's no more coffee.	You should ask the secretary for another.
5 Karl's computer keeps crashing.	You should call the engineer.
6 The photocopier's jammed.	You should take the bus.
7 My deadline is tomorrow.	He should call IT.
8 The metro isn't running tomorrow.	You should ask for an extension.

◀))

27.3 FILL IN THE GAPS USING THE WORDS IN THE PANEL

Susan _____misspelled_____ my name. It's Catherine with a "C."

1 Where have the reports gone? They've _____ .

2 Pete _____ me. He thought I said 3 o'clock.

3 Cathy isn't coming in today. She's feeling _____ .

4 You should be _____ crossing the road.

5 Doug is really _____ . He gets angry so easily.

6 I'm _____ to come to the training because I have a meeting.

7 Don't forget to _____ the machine after you've used it.

8 I'm _____ with that program. I don't know it.

9 Jean is so _____ . She's always making mistakes.

10 This morning is _____ for me. Can we meet later?

unable
impractical
careful
unfamiliar
~~misspelled~~
misunderstood
impatient
careless
disappeared
unwell
disconnect

◀))

27.4 CROSS OUT THE INCORRECT WORD IN EACH SENTENCE, THEN SAY THE SENTENCES OUT LOUD

What about arranging a meeting to discuss some practical / ~~impractical~~ solutions?

1 We should make sure no one understood / misunderstood the instructions.

2 How about organizing training for everyone who is unfamiliar / familiar with the program?

3 Let's make sure no one on the team spells / misspells the name wrongly again.

4 Why don't we ask Pete to help if Laura isn't well / unwell tomorrow?

5 I think we should disconnect / connect the machine since it's not working.

6 I don't think you should be so patient / impatient with the new recruits.

7 Let's send a memo to everyone who isn't able / unable to come to the meeting.

8 Let's explain to Tim that he should be more careful / careless with financial information.

9 Why don't we try to find a time that is convenient / inconvenient for everyone?

28 Giving a presentation

When you are preparing a presentation, make sure it is clear and easy to follow. There are certain phrases you can use to help guide the audience through the talk.

New language Signposting language
Aa Vocabulary Presentation equipment
New skill Structuring a talk

28.1 LISTEN TO THE AUDIO AND ANSWER THE QUESTIONS

The CEO of a clothing company is talking to her employees.

The presentation is about...
marketing. ☐ TV ads. ✓ websites. ☐

1 The speaker wants to focus on...
retired men. ☐ young adults. ☐ children. ☐

2 Young adults between 18 and 23 are buying...
sports wear. ☐ business wear. ☐ casual wear. ☐

3 Young adults between 24 and 30 buy more...
jackets. ☐ suits. ☐ sneakers. ☐

4 What percentage of Europeans wear sports wear?
50% ☐ 60% ☐ 65% ☐

5 What percentage of Americans wear sports wear?
70% ☐ 80% ☐ 85% ☐

6 The speaker is disappointed with growth in...
England. ☐ China. ☐ the US. ☐

7 The speaker hopes that growth will occur in...
South Africa. ☐ India. ☐ New Zealand. ☐

28.2 REWRITE THE SENTENCES, PUTTING THE WORDS IN THE CORRECT ORDER

we'll Next, benefits. explore the

Next, we'll explore the benefits.

1 about Today going I'm talk profit. to

_____

2 anyone questions? Does have any

_____

3 up, facing To we are issues. sum

_____

4 happy I'm to questions. answer

_____

5 the Last, look let's future. at

_____

◀))

91

28.3 MATCH THE BEGINNINGS OF THE SENTENCES TO THE CORRECT ENDINGS

Today, I want to talk	by showing you this graph.
① I'd like to begin	questions or comments?
② I'm happy to	about something really important.
③ Does anyone have any more	answer any questions.
④ Let's move	been an excellent quarter for the company.
⑤ After that, I would	on to the next topic.
⑥ To sum up, it's	like to talk about the merger.

Aa 28.4 FILL IN THE GAPS USING THE WORDS IN THE PANEL

Can you please look at the graph on your ___*handout*___ ?

① The _____ is black. We can't see the graph.

② If you use a _____ , you can introduce graphs and visuals.

③ I'll write down the company's name on the _____ .

④ There are programs to help you make professional-looking _____ .

⑤ If you use a _____ , the people at the back will hear you.

projector	slides	~~handout~~	flipchart	microphone	screen

28.5 CROSS OUT THE INCORRECT WORD IN EACH SENTENCE, THEN SAY THE SENTENCES OUT LOUD

Feel free to ask / ~~answer~~ any questions at the end.

1 I'd want / like to start with our factory in Vietnam.

2 To sum up / in, we need to invest more in infrastructure.

3 I'll explore / travel the benefits of investing in web technology later.

4 Let's begin in / by looking at the sales figures.

5 In short / small, we need to develop new products.

6 Let's take a look / view at the second graph.

7 So we've completed / covered all the topics I wanted to discuss.

8 Turning to / on the previous quarter's profits.

9 Then I'm going to talk / discuss about the situation in China.

10 For / To start, let's look at this year's performance.

11 Moving on / up, let's look at our main competitors.

12 First, I'm going to look at / in last year's results.

13 I'm happy to ask / answer any questions at the end.

14 I'd like to end in / by thanking you all for your attention today.

29 Rules and requests

Use "can" and "have to" to talk about rules in the workplace, and verbs such as "could" to politely ask colleagues to help you solve problems.

🔧 New language Modal verbs
Aa Vocabulary Polite requests
🧩 New skill Talking about rules and regulations

🔧 29.1 CROSS OUT THE INCORRECT WORDS IN EACH SENTENCE

There's a formal dress code here. You can't / ~~have to~~ wear shorts to work.

 1 You can't / don't have to stay late tonight. It's very quiet.

 2 Is your phone broken? You can / have to use mine if you like.

 3 We can't / have to wear a jacket and tie when we meet clients.

 4 You can't / don't have to park there. It's a space for disabled drivers.

🔊

🔧 29.2 MATCH THE BEGINNINGS OF THE STATEMENTS TO THE CORRECT ENDINGS

You have to turn off the lights. ──────→ It saves energy.

There's tea and coffee in the kitchen.

1 You can't leave early tonight.

2 You don't have to pay for lunch.

3 You can make yourself a hot drink.

That's the fire alarm.

There's a formal dress code.

4 We have to wear business clothes.

Staff eat for free in the cafeteria.

5 We have to leave the building now.

We have an important meeting at 5pm.

🔊

29.3 LISTEN TO THE AUDIO AND ANSWER THE QUESTIONS

Peter is having a difficult conversation with his manager.

Peter can take long lunch breaks.
True ☐ False ☐ Not given ☑

3 Women can't wear dresses to work.
True ☐ False ☐ Not given ☐

1 Staff can take their lunch break at 12:00.
True ☐ False ☐ Not given ☐

4 Men don't always have to wear a tie.
True ☐ False ☐ Not given ☐

2 Peter can wear jeans to work.
True ☐ False ☐ Not given ☐

5 Staff don't have to clean up the meeting rooms.
True ☐ False ☐ Not given ☐

29.4 REWRITE THE SENTENCES, CORRECTING THE ERRORS

I has to stay late tonight. There's so much to do!
I have to stay late tonight. There's so much to do!

1 I can to listen to music at work if I use headphones.

_____

2 He's a pilot. He have to wear a uniform.

_____

3 They doesn't has to go to the training session.

_____

4 He can't taking more than an hour for his lunch break.

_____

5 He doesn't have to leave early. It's too busy.

_____

6 I have back up my files before I turn my computer off.

_____

29.5 MATCH THE PICTURES TO THE CORRECT SENTENCES

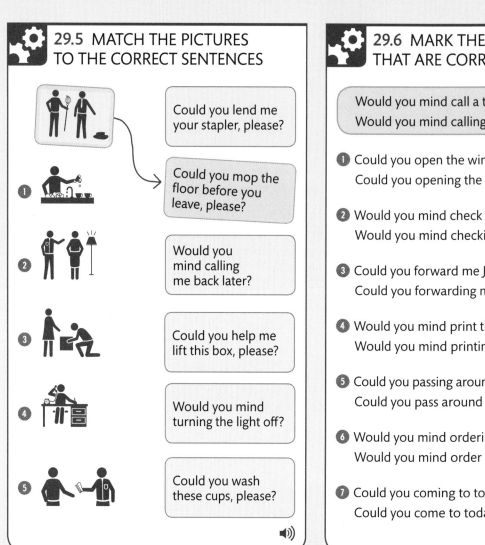

Could you lend me your stapler, please?

Could you mop the floor before you leave, please?

Would you mind calling me back later?

Could you help me lift this box, please?

Would you mind turning the light off?

Could you wash these cups, please?

29.6 MARK THE REQUESTS THAT ARE CORRECT

Would you mind call a taxi? ☐
Would you mind calling a taxi? ☑

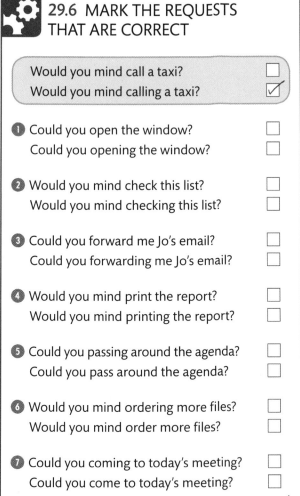

1 Could you open the window? ☐
   Could you opening the window? ☐

2 Would you mind check this list? ☐
   Would you mind checking this list? ☐

3 Could you forward me Jo's email? ☐
   Could you forwarding me Jo's email? ☐

4 Would you mind print the report? ☐
   Would you mind printing the report? ☐

5 Could you passing around the agenda? ☐
   Could you pass around the agenda? ☐

6 Would you mind ordering more files? ☐
   Would you mind order more files? ☐

7 Could you coming to today's meeting? ☐
   Could you come to today's meeting? ☐

29.7 WRITE EACH SENTENCE IN ITS OTHER FORM

Could you make us tea and coffee?	Would you mind making us tea and coffee?
1	Would you mind turning your music down?
2 Could you check my report for me?	
3	Would you mind closing the window?
4 Could you invite Alan to the meeting?	

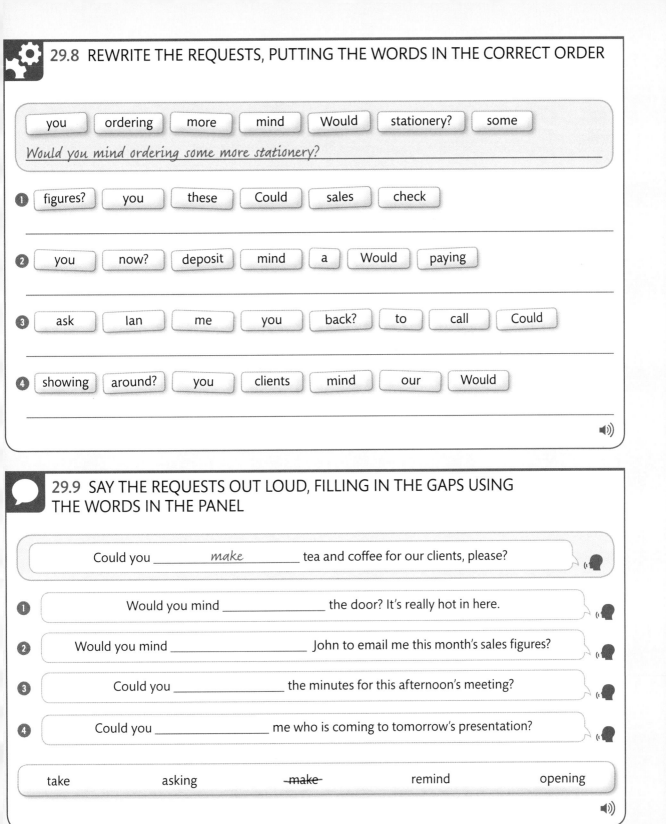

29.8 REWRITE THE REQUESTS, PUTTING THE WORDS IN THE CORRECT ORDER

| you | ordering | more | mind | Would | stationery? | some |

Would you mind ordering some more stationery?

❶ | figures? | you | these | Could | sales | check |

_____

❷ | you | now? | deposit | mind | a | Would | paying |

_____

❸ | ask | Ian | me | you | back? | to | call | Could |

_____

❹ | showing | around? | you | clients | mind | our | Would |

_____

29.9 SAY THE REQUESTS OUT LOUD, FILLING IN THE GAPS USING THE WORDS IN THE PANEL

Could you _____*make*_____ tea and coffee for our clients, please?

❶ Would you mind _____ the door? It's really hot in here.

❷ Would you mind _____ John to email me this month's sales figures?

❸ Could you _____ the minutes for this afternoon's meeting?

❹ Could you _____ me who is coming to tomorrow's presentation?

| take | asking | ~~make~~ | remind | opening |

30 Vocabulary

Aa 30.1 WORK IDIOMS WRITE THE PHRASES FROM THE PANEL UNDER THE CORRECT DEFINITIONS

To start something

to get the ball rolling

1 To think about something in an original way

_____

3 Administration, paperwork, or rules and regulations

4 To relax or calm down

_____

6 To gradually relax

7 The normal daily routine at a company

_____

9 A situation with no negative outcome

10 To owe money

_____

12 It is your turn to do or say something

13 To delay or avoid something

_____

15 Wasting money

16 To be really busy

_____

2 To start work on something that needs doing

_____

5 To be busy doing something else

_____

8 To not be working

_____

11 To work very long hours

_____

14 Not acting or behaving as it should

_____

17 To do a fair share of work

_____

to work around the clock   going haywire

to be out of order   ~~to get the ball rolling~~

to think outside the box   to take it easy

throwing money down the drain   red tape

to pull your weight   to be in the red

a win-win situation   to be swamped

to wind down   the ball is in your court

business as usual   to get down to business

to be tied up with   to put something off

31 Discussing issues

Many common workplace problems arise from an ongoing situation in the past. You can use the past continuous tense to discuss these problems.

⚙ **New language** Past continuous
Aa Vocabulary Work idioms
🧩 **New skill** Describing workplace problems

⚙ **31.1 MARK THE SENTENCES THAT ARE CORRECT**

Chris weren't answering his phone. ☐
Chris wasn't answering his phone. ☑

❶ Tanya was feeling very tired. ☐
Tanya were feeling very tired. ☐

❷ I were finishing his report. ☐
I was finishing his report. ☐

❸ Alison was talk to the CEO. ☐
Alison was talking to the CEO. ☐

❹ Was Jamie taking minutes? ☐
Were Jamie taking minutes? ☐

❺ Was you working late yesterday? ☐
Were you working late yesterday? ☐

❻ I trying was to call you. ☐
I was trying to call you. ☐

❼ Claire were playing very loud music. ☐
Claire was playing very loud music. ☐

🔊

⚙ **31.2 FILL IN THE GAPS BY PUTTING THE VERBS IN THE PAST CONTINUOUS**

My computer ___wasn't working___ (not work) this morning.

❶ The train trip here was really bad. All the trains _____ (run) late.

❷ The cleaners _____ (complain) that staff left their dirty cups in the sink.

❸ Harriet _____ (not listen) to the presentation.

❹ Tom's manager was annoyed because Tom _____ (not meet) his deadlines.

❺ My email inbox _____ (get) full, so I had to delete some messages.

🔊

31.3 LISTEN TO THE AUDIO AND ANSWER THE QUESTIONS

 Alina and Howard are talking about a difficult morning at work.

Alina finished her report this morning.
True ☐ **False** ☑

❸ Alina has the sales figures that she needs.
True ☐ **False** ☐

❶ Howard's laptop wasn't working.
True ☐ **False** ☐

❹ Howard thinks the report needs a new approach.
True ☐ **False** ☐

❷ IT solved the problem with Howard's computer.
True ☐ **False** ☐

❺ They don't have a computer that they can use.
True ☐ **False** ☐

31.4 DESCRIBE THE PICTURES OUT LOUD, USING THE WORDS IN THE PANEL TO FILL IN THE GAPS

The printer ___wasn't___ ___working___ yesterday.

❸ Lucia _____ the minutes of the meeting.

❶ Joshua _____ a talk about new markets.

❹ They _____ too loudly on the phone.

❷ Fiona _____ to Bilal's new ideas for products.

❺ Helen _____ her lunch at her desk.

wasn't listening	was eating	were speaking	was giving	~~wasn't working~~	was taking

Louise's Blog

HOME | ENTRIES | ABOUT | CONTACT

Having a bad day at work is something that happens to all of us. Delayed trains, co-workers who annoy you, printers that don't work; it all adds up to stress for the best of us.

Take last week, for example. I missed an important meeting with a new supplier. My boss was sick, so I had to go instead, but my train was running late. I also had a cold because my co-workers were always leaving the windows next to the fire doors and the elevators open. To make matters worse, the people in my pod were talking really loudly and it was hard to concentrate. I knew it was Ben's last day and that they were having drinks and snacks to say goodbye, but I had lots of work to do.

Later that week, I had a long meeting with my boss. I tried to tell him that it didn't help that my assistant was copying me into lots of emails I didn't need to see. My boss said I needed to talk to my assistant and ask him to talk to me first if he was unsure of anything. I felt better after my update meeting, but when I got back to my desk, my USB cable and headphones were missing. Someone was borrowing them without asking. This was always happening. I was fed up.

So what should you do when you have a week like mine? When everything is going haywire, talking to a co-worker for ten minutes can help. It's good to share problems, but don't turn it into a complaining session. Complaining is negative and uses up our energy. Having a quick walk outside should clear your head. Our bodies like to be in the open air and sunlight for half an hour a day, so go for a walk after lunch instead of reading those reports. Then you can tackle a full inbox with a positive perspective.

Why did Louise miss her meeting? **She was sick** ☐ **It was canceled** ☐ **Her train was running late** ☑

❶ What were Louise's co-workers always opening? **The windows** ☐ **The doors** ☐ **The elevators** ☐

❷ How were Louise's co-workers making it difficult for her to focus? **Talking** ☐ **Eating** ☐ **Drinking** ☐

❸ Who was sending Louise too many emails? **Her boss** ☐ **Her assistant** ☐ **Her co-workers** ☐

❹ What was missing from Louise's desk? **Her laptop** ☐ **Her files** ☐ **Her USB cable** ☐

❺ What should you do if you're stressed? **Complain** ☐ **Talk to a co-worker** ☐ **Use up energy** ☐

❻ What does Louise say a walk outside can help us do? **Think clearly** ☐ **Get fit** ☐ **Enjoy nature** ☐

32 Apologies and explanations

English uses a variety of polite phrases to apologize for mistakes. Use the past continuous with the past simple to offer an explanation for a mistake.

⚙ **New language** Past continuous and past simple
Aa Vocabulary Workplace mistakes
🛠 **New skill** Apologizing and giving explanations

32.1 MARK THE SENTENCES THAT ARE CORRECT

I like to apologize for keeping you waiting so long. ☐
I would like to apologize for keeping you waiting so long. ☑

1. I am so sorry I was late for the meeting with our clients today. ☐
   I so sorry I was late for the meeting with our clients today. ☐

2. I would like to apologize for not finish the report yesterday. ☐
   I would like to apologize for not finishing the report yesterday. ☐

3. I'm sorry really. I forgot to charge the office cell phone and it has no power. ☐
   I'm really sorry. I forgot to charge the office cell phone and it has no power. ☐

4. I'm really apologize this line is so bad. I hope we don't get cut off. ☐
   I'm really sorry this line is so bad. I hope we don't get cut off. ☐

5. I'm afraid that's not enough good. I want a full refund on my ticket. ☐
   I'm afraid that's not good enough. I want a full refund on my ticket. ☐

🔊

Aa 32.2 MATCH THE APOLOGIES WITH THE CORRECT RESPONSES

I'm very sorry if the waiter was rude. ——→ That's all right. I could see he was very busy.

1. I'm so sorry. My presentation isn't ready. — No problem. I'll help you finish it now.

2. I apologize if your food was cold. — That's not good enough. Please heat it up.

3. I'm really sorry, but I have to leave early. — Don't worry. I'll print off some more.

4. I'm very sorry the coffee machine's broken. — Never mind. We're not very busy today.

5. I'm really sorry. I left the reports at home. — No problem. I'll have tea instead.

🔊

32.3 LISTEN TO THE AUDIO, THEN NUMBER THE PICTURES IN THE ORDER THEY ARE DESCRIBED

A ☐   B ☐   C 1   D ☐   E ☐

32.4 SAY THE SENTENCES OUT LOUD, FILLING IN THE GAPS USING THE WORDS IN THE PANEL

I really ___must___ apologize for not calling you back earlier.

4 That's all _____ . I'll make you a copy right now.

1 I'm really _____ . I forgot to send the agenda for the meeting.

5 Please _____ sure it doesn't happen again.

2 I would like to _____ for the rudeness of the waitress.

6 Never _____ . It's only a cup.

3 I'm _____ that's not good enough. You missed an important meeting.

7 I would _____ to apologize for the delay to your train this evening.

| ~~must~~ | like | mind | apologize | sorry | afraid | make | right |

104

32.5 CROSS OUT THE INCORRECT WORDS IN EACH SENTENCE

> I ~~wrote~~ / was writing a report when my computer crashed / ~~was crashing~~.

1 Harry practiced / was practicing his presentation when I called / was calling him.

2 Sam's cell phone rang / was ringing when Tom described / was describing the sales for this quarter.

3 The elevator got / was getting stuck while they waited / were waiting for it.

4 Tina didn't listen / wasn't listening when the CEO said / was saying all staff would get a raise.

5 The fire alarm went / was going off when we had / were having our update meeting.

6 I worked / was working late when I heard / was hearing a strange noise.

7 I edited / was editing the report when the fire alarm went / was going off.

32.6 FILL IN THE GAPS BY PUTTING THE VERBS IN THE PAST CONTINUOUS OR PAST SIMPLE

> I ___was driving___ (🚗 drive) to a meeting when someone ___crashed___ (🚗 crash) into me.

1 The photocopier _____ (🖨 break) while I _____ (🖨 copy) your sales report.

2 We _____ (📊 listen) to Janet's presentation when the power _____ (📊 go) off.

3 John _____ (✈ sign) the contract when the lawyer _____ (📞 call) him.

4 Anna _____ (😠 be) furious when she found out George _____ (👥 copy) her ideas.

5 Simon _____ (💻 edit) the report when his computer _____ (💻 crash).

6 We _____ (🚏 wait) for the bus when two buses _____ (🚌 arrive).

33 Tasks and targets

When you are dealing with deadlines and pressure at work, you can use the present perfect to let your co-workers know how your work is progressing.

New language Present perfect and past simple
Aa Vocabulary Workplace tasks
New skill Discussing achievements at work

33.1 FILL IN THE GAPS BY PUTTING THE VERBS IN THE PRESENT PERFECT

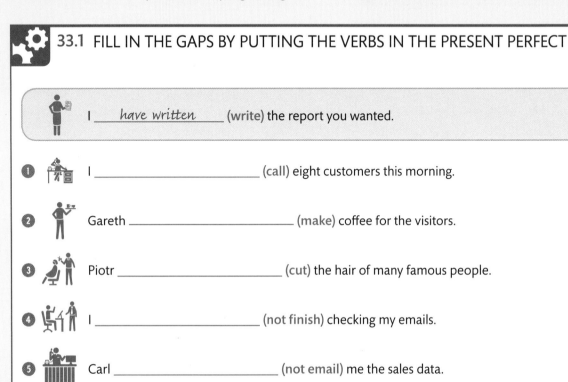

I _____ *have written* _____ (write) the report you wanted.

① I _____ (call) eight customers this morning.

② Gareth _____ (make) coffee for the visitors.

③ Piotr _____ (cut) the hair of many famous people.

④ I _____ (not finish) checking my emails.

⑤ Carl _____ (not email) me the sales data.

33.2 CROSS OUT THE INCORRECT WORD IN EACH SENTENCE

I've just / ~~yet~~ sent him the files.

① She hasn't sent the invoice just / yet.

② We have yet / just heard the CEO is leaving.

③ I haven't met the new director yet / just.

④ Has Tom finished fixing my laptop just / yet?

⑤ George has just / yet called me.

⑥ The painters haven't finished yet / just.

⑦ Have you had a meeting with Ann yet / just?

⑧ The trainer has just / yet arrived.

⑨ Have you just / yet finished the report?

33.3 REWRITE THE SENTENCES, PUTTING THE WORDS IN THE CORRECT ORDER

just | preparing | have | my | I | presentation. | finished

I have just finished preparing my presentation.

1. the | haven't | stationery | yet. | I | ordered

   _____

2. the | They | packaging. | just | new | introduced | have

   _____

3. answered | you | emails | yet? | those | Have

   _____

4. our | minutes | has | written | from | Derinda | the | meeting. | just

   _____

33.4 READ LAILA'S TO DO LIST AND ANSWER THE QUESTIONS

Laila has emailed the CEO.
True ☐ **False** ☐ **Not given** ☑

1. Laila has organized the team meeting.
   True ☐ **False** ☐ **Not given** ☐

2. Laila has photocopied the expenses claims.
   True ☐ **False** ☐ **Not given** ☐

3. Laila hasn't updated the database.
   True ☐ **False** ☐ **Not given** ☐

4. Accounts has found the missing invoice.
   True ☐ **False** ☐ **Not given** ☐

To do list

- ~~Organize team meeting~~
- ~~Write FAQs for new staff~~
- Photocopy boss's expenses claims
- Update the database
- ~~Call Accounts about missing invoice~~
- Get bus timetables for visitors

33.5 REWRITE THE SENTENCES, CORRECTING THE ERRORS

Tim has given a great presentation yesterday afternoon.
Tim gave a great presentation yesterday afternoon.

1 Daniel has sent your package last Friday.

_____

2 Jenny has shown me the new designs yesterday.

_____

3 Babu and Zack hasn't finished their research yet.

_____

4 Kate has spoken to the HR manager last week.

_____

33.6 LISTEN TO THE AUDIO AND MARK WHICH THINGS ACTUALLY HAPPENED

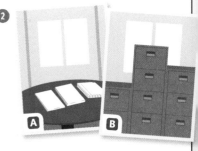

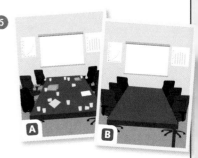

33.7 MARK THE SENTENCES THAT ARE CORRECT

I've finished the reports last week. ☐
I finished the reports last week. ☑

1. I has done all the invoices for June. ☐
   I have done all the invoices for June. ☐

2. He met the Chinese partners last month. ☐
   He has met the Chinese partners last month. ☐

3. He hasn't sent the salaries to payroll yet. ☐
   He hasn't sended the salaries to payroll yet. ☐

4. They not started the audit yet. ☐
   They have not started the audit yet. ☐

5. He has left this morning. ☐
   He left this morning. ☐

6. I have yet heard about your promotion. ☐
   I have just heard about your promotion. ☐

7. She have sold the most products. ☐
   She has sold the most products. ☐

8. Have you designed that box yet? ☐
   You have designed that box yet? ☐

9. They have given him a verbal warning. ☐
   They have gived him a verbal warning. ☐

10. Mark hasn't scanned it just. ☐
    Mark hasn't scanned it yet. ☐

11. I have speaked to your team. ☐
    I have spoken to your team. ☐

◀))

33.8 RESPOND OUT LOUD TO THE AUDIO, FILLING IN THE GAPS USING THE WORDS IN THE PANEL

Have you finished the reports?

No, I haven't finished them _yet._

3. Where are the contracts?

_____ filed them all in the cabinet.

1. Have you scanned the photos?

Yes, I've _____ scanned them.

4. Why are there no newspapers?

We've _____ the delivery.

2. Has Philip audited the books?

No, he _____ done them yet.

I've   just   stopped
   hasn't   ~~yet~~

◀))

34 Dealing with complaints

If a customer complains about a problem, one way to offer a solution, and to make predictions or promises, is to use the future with "will."

⚙️ **New language** The future with "will"
Aa Vocabulary Complaints and apologies
🧩 **New skill** Dealing with complaints

34.1 MARK THE SENTENCES THAT ARE CORRECT

The company wills offer you a discount. ☐
The company will offer you a discount. ☑

❶ We will replace your tablet free of charge. ☐
We will to replace your tablet free of charge. ☐

❷ The chef will cooks you another pizza. ☐
The chef will cook you another pizza. ☐

❸ I'll talk to the boss about it. ☐
I'll talking to the boss about it. ☐

❹ The manager be will with you soon. ☐
The manager will be with you soon. ☐

❺ I contact our courier immediately. ☐
I'll contact our courier immediately. ☐

❻ We will give you a full refund. ☐
We will to give you a full refund. ☐

❼ I promise that your order arrive today. ☐
I promise that your order will arrive today. ☐

❽ I'm afraid we won't finish the project on time. ☐
I'm afraid we willn't finish the project on time. ☐

❾ I'm sorry, but we don't will cancel your order. ☐
I'm sorry, but we won't cancel your order. ☐

🔊

34.2 MATCH THE COMPLAINTS TO THE CORRECT RESPONSES

My bus was three hours late.

❶ My luggage didn't arrive.

❷ This food is cold.

❸ You have charged me twice.

❹ I've been waiting for a taxi for 40 minutes.

❺ There is no hot water in our bathroom.

We'll move you to another room.

I will call the driver immediately.

We'll refund you the price of your ticket.

We'll send it to your hotel when it gets here.

I'll ask the chef to cook it properly.

I'll refund the money to your credit card.

🔊

Dear Mr. Vance,

Thank you for your letter of March 3. I am sorry to hear you were not happy with the service provided by our hotel during your two-day business trip to Rome last month. First of all, I sincerely apologize that there was no receptionist when you arrived at midnight. We will ask our receptionists to work late when travelers are delayed so that there is always someone to welcome our guests in the future. I am also sorry to hear that the bathroom in your hotel suite had not been cleaned. I agree that this was unacceptable, and I will speak to the cleaning services manager. Regarding breakfast, I am sorry that there was no bread and that you had to ask for hot coffee. I will speak to the catering staff to ensure this does not happen again. With reference to the hotel's policy on guaranteeing residents a good night's sleep, I am so sorry to hear that you were kept awake by guests in the adjoining room. Given all the above, I would like to offer a full refund of what you paid for your two-night hotel stay.

I hope this is satisfactory.
Yours sincerely,
Mr. J Silvano

Why did Mr. Vance write to the hotel?
To complain about the food in Rome ☐
To thank them for a pleasant stay ☐
To complain about his stay there ☑

❶ What was the problem when Mr. Vance checked in?
The security guard arrived after midnight ☐
The security guard was rude ☐
There was no receptionist ☐

❷ What will the hotel do in the future?
They will ask receptionists to work late ☐
Receptionists will go to the airport ☐
Receptionists will not work late ☐

❸ What was wrong with Mr. Vance's hotel suite?
It was noisy at night ☐
The light didn't work ☐
The bathroom was dirty ☐

❹ How will this complaint be addressed?
Mr. Silvano will clean the bathrooms ☐
Mr. Silvano will apologize to the cleaner. ☐
He will speak to the cleaners' manager ☐

❺ What was wrong with the breakfast?
There wasn't any hot coffee ☐
There wasn't any juice ☐
There wasn't any cereal ☐

❻ What was the problem that evening?
Mr. Vance had to work late ☐
Mr. Vance went to a party ☐
Mr. Vance was kept awake ☐

❼ What does Mr. Silvano offer Mr. Vance?
A discount off his next stay ☐
A full refund ☐
A refund for one night's stay in the hotel ☐

34.4 REWRITE THE SENTENCES, PUTTING THE WORDS IN THE CORRECT ORDER

| in | arrive | minutes? | next | Will | the | ten | train | the |

Will the train arrive in the next ten minutes?

① | next | you | stay. | a | hotel | discount | offer | We'll | your | off |

_____

② | to | refunded | the | card? | money | Will | credit | be | my |

_____

③ | your | chase | The | order | you. | will | up | for | company |

_____

④ | with | will | very | The | you | manager | soon. | be | store |

_____

⑤ | the | washing | Will | machine? | broken | on | part | my | replace | you |

_____

🔊

34.5 LISTEN TO THE AUDIO AND MARK WHETHER EACH SCENARIO WILL OR WON'T HAPPEN TODAY

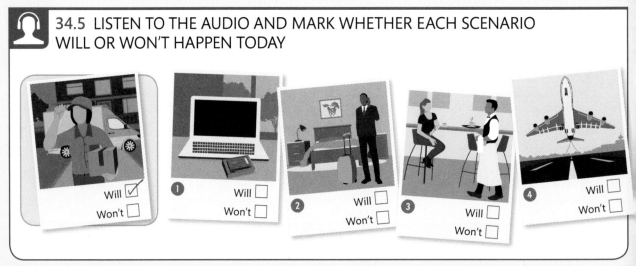

Will ☑
Won't ☐

① Will ☐
Won't ☐

② Will ☐
Won't ☐

③ Will ☐
Won't ☐

④ Will ☐
Won't ☐

My train was an hour late.

I do apologize. We _'ll refund_ the fare to your credit card.

1 The concert was canceled when we got to the venue last night.

I'm very sorry about that. _____ you a refund.

2 My pasta is cold.

I really must apologize. I _____ it back to the kitchen.

3 Where is the sales assistant? I want to try these shoes on.

She _____ with you in a minute.

4 The receptionist was rude.

I _____ to her about this.

5 Your assistant didn't finish that report I asked him to prepare.

It _____ again.

6 There aren't any vegetarian options on this menu.

I _____ the chef to make you something vegetarian.

won't happen   'll take   'll refund   'll ask   We'll offer   'll be   'll talk

Aa **35.1 TRANSPORTATION** WRITE THE WORDS FROM THE PANEL UNDER THE CORRECT PICTURES

metro

1 _____

2 _____

3 _____

4 _____

5 _____

6 _____

7 _____

8 _____

9 _____

10 _____

11 _____

| car | taxi | bus stop | train station | bus | helicopter |
| tram | taxi stand (US) / taxi rank (UK) | airport | ~~metro~~ | bicycle | plane |

one-way ticket

1 _____

2 _____

3 _____

4 _____

5 _____

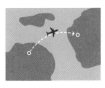
6 _____

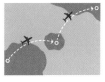
7 _____

8 _____

9 _____

10 _____

11 _____

12 _____

13 _____

14 _____

15 _____

16 _____

17 _____

18 _____

19 _____

passport   aisle seat   terminal   passport control   board a plane   check-in   ~~one-way ticket~~

international flight   round-trip ticket (US) / return ticket (UK)   window seat   late   boarding pass

on time   domestic flight   delay   luggage   connecting flight   seat reservation   security   hotel

36 Making travel arrangements

When you have travel plans or want to discuss the arrangements for a trip, it is useful to be able to talk about the possible results of actions and choices.

✿ **New language** Zero and first conditional
Aa Vocabulary Travel
✦ **New skill** Talking about actions and results

 36.1 FILL IN THE GAPS BY PUTTING THE VERBS IN THE CORRECT TENSES TO MAKE SENTENCES IN THE FIRST CONDITIONAL

> If you _____book_____ (book) in advance, you _____will get_____ (get) a discount.

1 If we _____ (not hurry) , we _____ (miss) the flight.

2 If we _____ (meet) in Berlin, it _____ (save) us some time.

3 We _____ (take) on a new intern if we _____ (win) the contract.

4 If the train _____ (be) late, we _____ (miss) the meeting.

5 If the bank _____ (be) closed, we _____ (not have) any money.

6 We _____ (pay) for your flight if you _____ (fly) to Denver.

7 If you _____ (work) hard, you _____ (pass) the exam.

8 The firm _____ (pay) expenses if you _____ (be) delayed.

9 If I _____ (go) to Rome, I _____ (visit) the Colosseum.

10 If I _____ (lose) my job, I don't know what I _____ (do).

◀))

36.2 MATCH THE BEGINNINGS OF THE SENTENCES TO THE CORRECT ENDINGS

We will win the contract → if we negotiate effectively.

1. If we don't hurry up, — we'll miss our connecting flight.

2. We will get a discount — if we book early.

3. Will you pay expenses — we will have to lay Sean off.

4. What will Samantha do if — if you go to China?

5. If we lose the contract, — if we attend the conference?

6. Will you visit the factory — she loses her job next month?

◀))

36.3 MARK THE SENTENCES THAT ARE CORRECT

If the flight is delayed, we will definitely miss the meeting. ☑
If the flight will be delayed, we definitely miss the meeting. ☐

1. Will you have a celebration if you get the job? ☐
   Do you have a celebration if you get the job? ☐

2. If you'll buy the ticket online, it will be cheaper. ☐
   If you buy the ticket online, it will be cheaper. ☐

3. If we visit Paris, we probably go sightseeing. ☐
   If we visit Paris, we will probably go sightseeing. ☐

4. What will we do if we don't win the contract? ☐
   What do we do if we won't win the contract? ☐

5. If we'll take on a new intern, where do they sit? ☐
   If we take on a new intern, where will they sit? ☐

6. How will you travel to Berlin if the flight is canceled? ☐
   How do you travel to Berlin if the flight will be canceled? ☐

◀))

36.4 LISTEN TO THE AUDIO AND ANSWER THE QUESTIONS

Clara is speaking to Jane on the phone in order to sort out the details of an upcoming trip.

② They both agree to take a taxi.
True ☐ False ☐ Not given ☐

③ The Hotel Ritz is more expensive.
True ☐ False ☐ Not given ☐

④ The Hotel Grande is closer to the convention hall.
True ☐ False ☐ Not given ☐

Clara has already booked the flights.
True ☐ False ☑ Not given ☐

⑤ The Hotel Ritz includes breakfast.
True ☐ False ☐ Not given ☐

❶ If they book the flights online, they will be cheaper.
True ☐ False ☐ Not given ☐

⑥ The company will pay for all meals.
True ☐ False ☐ Not given ☐

36.5 REWRITE THE SENTENCES, PUTTING THE WORDS IN THE CORRECT ORDER

| pay | travel | to | class, | you | more. | If | you | first | have |

If you travel first class, you have to pay more.

❶ | If | to | nice | work. | walk | it's | a | day, | I |

_____

❷ | water, | If | heat | it | boils. | you |

_____

❸ | for | late | boss | isn't | work, | you're | If | unhappy? | your |

_____

❹ | that | press | If | machine | button, | the | you | stops. |

_____

◀))

36.6 CROSS OUT THE INCORRECT WORDS IN EACH SENTENCE, THEN SAY THE SENTENCES OUT LOUD

If you press / ~~will press~~ the red button here, the machine stops immediately.

1. Will you visit Red Square if you go / will go to Moscow?

2. People use public transportation if it is / be cheap.

3. What will we do if we lose / will lose the contract?

4. The ticket will be / is more expensive if we buy it later.

5. If you pay / will pay staff more, they work harder.

6. Will / Do you pick me up from the station if I give you my details?

7. We'll miss the train if we won't / don't hurry.

8. If it rains / will rain, the event is always moved indoors.

9. Sharon won't / doesn't go on vacation if she loses her job.

10. Does / Will Doug resign if the company loses the deal?

37 Asking for directions

When traveling to conferences and meetings, you may need to ask for directions. Knowing how to be polite but clear is essential.

🔧 **New language** Imperatives, prepositions of place
Aa Vocabulary Directions
🧩 **New skill** Asking for and giving directions

37.1 CROSS OUT THE INCORRECT WORD IN EACH SENTENCE

 Go past the café and ~~turning~~ / turn left.

1 Do you know the where / way to the station?

2 The bank is in / on the corner.

3 Do you know how to go / get to the hotel?

4 The museum is on / in front of the park.

5 You should take / make the second left.

6 The library is straight ahead on the / a right.

7 Our house is just ahead on / in the left.

8 Sorry, did you tell / say it is near the school?

9 Turn right on / at the sign.

🔊

37.2 MARK THE SENTENCES THAT ARE CORRECT

The office is 30 yards ahead on the right. ☑
The office is 30 yards ahead by the right. ☐

1 The entrance is in front of the factory. ☐
The entrance is on front of the factory. ☐

2 Turn right in the sign. ☐
Turn right at the sign. ☐

3 The bank is opposite the school. ☐
The bank is between the school. ☐

4 Take the first road in the left. ☐
Take the first road on the left. ☐

5 Go past the movie theater. ☐
Go after the movie theater. ☐

6 The bank is on the corner. ☐
The bank is at the corner. ☐

7 The station is next in the police station. ☐
The station is next to the police station. ☐

🔊

37.3 REWRITE THE SENTENCES, PUTTING THE WORDS IN THE CORRECT ORDER

| conference | the | of | The | city | is | in | hall. | front | center |

The conference center is in front of the city hall.

① | do | to | Excuse | you | the | know | way | the | hotel? | me, |

_____

② | it's | the | and | train | station. | straight | Go | opposite | on |

_____

③ | next | post | Sorry, | you | the | say | it's | office? | did | to |

_____

④ | the | yards | corner. | The | on | 40 | ahead | bank | is |

_____

◀))

37.4 LISTEN TO THE AUDIO AND MARK THE DIRECTIONS GIVEN

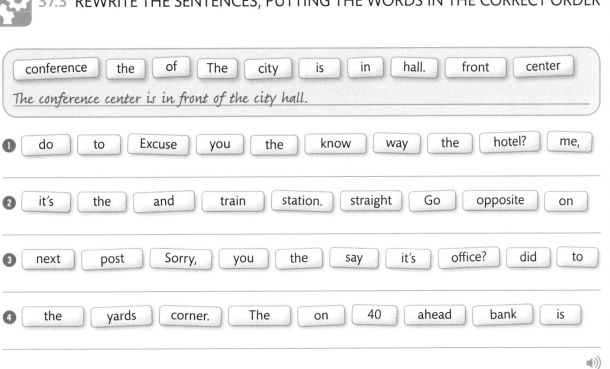

37.5 LOOK AT THE MAP THEN ANSWER THE QUESTIONS, SPEAKING OUT LOUD

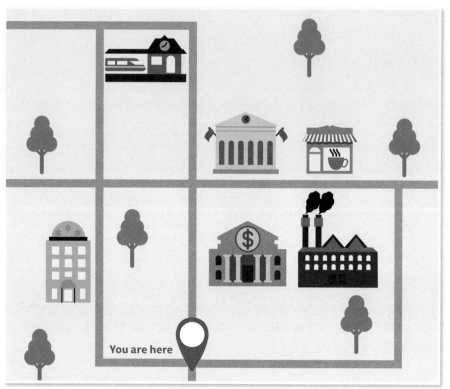

You are here

Do you know the way to the town hall?

Yes, turn right after the bank.

❶ How do I get to the café?

❷ Could you tell me the way to the train station?

❸ Do you know where I can find a bank?

❹ Do you know where the factory is?

❺ Where is the closest hotel to here?

38 Describing your stay

You can describe events using either active or passive sentences. The focus in a passive sentence is on the action itself rather than the thing that caused it.

⚙ **New language** The passive voice
Aa Vocabulary Hotels and accommodation
🧩 **New skill** Using the passive voice

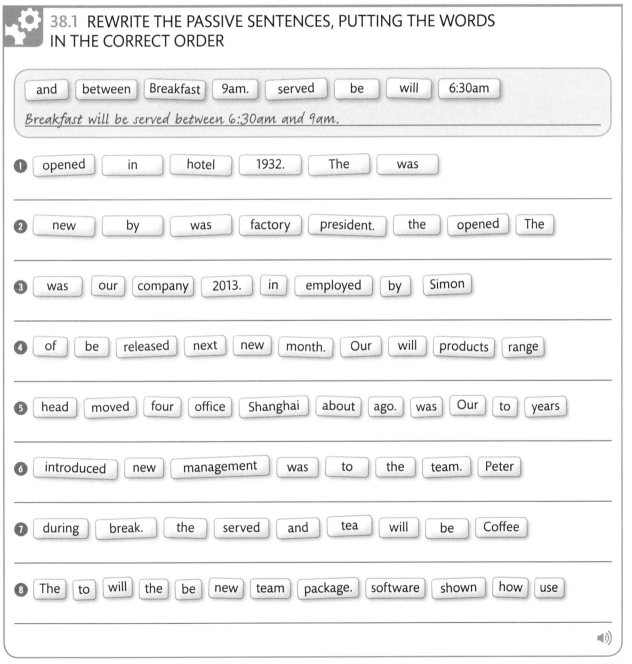

38.1 REWRITE THE PASSIVE SENTENCES, PUTTING THE WORDS IN THE CORRECT ORDER

and | between | Breakfast | 9am. | served | be | will | 6:30am

Breakfast will be served between 6:30am and 9am.

① opened | in | hotel | 1932. | The | was

② new | by | was | factory | president. | the | opened | The

③ was | our | company | 2013. | in | employed | by | Simon

④ of | be | released | next | new | month. | Our | will | products | range

⑤ head | moved | four | office | Shanghai | about | ago. | was | Our | to | years

⑥ introduced | new | management | was | to | the | team. | Peter

⑦ during | break. | the | served | and | tea | will | be | Coffee

⑧ The | to | will | the | be | new | team | package. | software | shown | how | use

🔊

123

38.2 REWRITE THE ACTIVE SENTENCES AS PASSIVE SENTENCES

| Someone moved the photocopier last night. | = | *The photocopier was moved last night.* |

1. Someone met the CEO at the airport. = _____
2. Danny has redecorated the meeting room. = _____
3. My assistant booked a double room yesterday. = _____
4. Julia taught the team some Mandarin. = _____
5. Someone left the files on the train again. = _____
6. John booked the rooms on Monday. = _____
7. The hotel serves breakfast at 7:30am. = _____
8. Someone has organized the office. = _____

38.3 LISTEN TO THE AUDIO, THEN NUMBER THE PICTURES IN THE ORDER THEY ARE DESCRIBED

38.4 READ THE REVIEWS AND ANSWER THE QUESTIONS

The reviewer thinks Hotel Destiny is expensive.
True ☐ **False** ☐ **Not given** ☑

1 The reviewer took a taxi to Hotel Destiny.
True ☐ **False** ☐ **Not given** ☐

2 There are conference facilities at Hotel Destiny.
True ☐ **False** ☐ **Not given** ☐

3 The television at Hotel Belvedere did not work.
True ☐ **False** ☐ **Not given** ☐

4 The receptionist was helpful at Hotel Belvedere.
True ☐ **False** ☐ **Not given** ☐

Hotels etc

Hotel Destiny ★ ★ ★ ★
This hotel is comfortable and affordable. It's perfect if you're staying in Shanghai for work or a short break. My colleague and I were picked up by the hotel minibus from the airport. After checking in, we looked around the hotel: there is a small restaurant, a gym in the basement, and a karaoke bar. Great fun!

Hotel Belvedere ★
We had been told that this is one of the best hotels in the area, but what we found proved shocking. The TV didn't turn on, and the bed fell apart on the second night. When I went downstairs to complain, I was ignored by the receptionist, and finally my wife and I were forced to check out three days early.

38.5 RESPOND OUT LOUD TO THE AUDIO, FILLING IN THE GAPS USING THE PHRASES IN THE PANEL

How was your flight?

The flight _____*was delayed*_____ by eight hours.

1 How did you get to the hotel?

We _____ at the airport by the driver.

2 How was the breakfast?

Great. It _____ at 7am each morning.

3 Was there a TV in the room?

Yes. But unfortunately it _____ .

| was broken | were picked up | ~~was delayed~~ | was served |

Aa 39.1 EATING OUT WRITE THE WORDS FROM THE PANEL UNDER THE CORRECT PICTURES

restaurant

1 _____

2 _____

3 _____

4 _____

5 _____

6 _____

7 _____

8 _____

9 _____

10 _____

11 _____

12 _____

13 _____

14 _____

15 _____

16 _____

17 _____

18 _____

19 _____

menu	vegan	vegetarian	boil	waitress	~~restaurant~~	roast	fry
lunch	café	food allergy / intolerance		tip		waiter	receipt
bar	chef	dessert	breakfast	make a reservation / booking			dinner

soup

❶ _____

❷ _____

❸ _____

❹ _____

❺ _____

❻ _____

❼ _____

❽ _____

❾ _____

❿ _____

⓫ _____

⓬ _____

⓭ _____

⓮ _____

⓯ _____

⓰ _____

⓱ _____

⓲ _____

⓳ _____

fruit	napkin	fork	tea	bread	~~soup~~	coffee
pasta	seafood	vegetables	salad	fish	milk	cake
meat	water	sandwich	knife	butter	potatoes

127

40 Conferences and visitors

Whether you are welcoming visitors, or visiting somewhere on business yourself, it is important to know how to interact politely in English.

⚙ **New language** "A," "some," "any"
Aa Vocabulary Hospitality
🧩 **New skill** Welcoming visitors

⚙ 40.1 MARK THE SENTENCES THAT ARE CORRECT

Welcome to China, Mr. Arnold. ☑
Welcome in China, Mr. Arnold. ☐

❶ Did you have any trouble getting here? ☐
Did you have any trouble arriving here? ☐

❷ Can I serve you anything? ☐
Can I get you anything? ☐

❸ It's great to meet you on person. ☐
It's great to meet you in person. ☐

❹ Have you been to Toronto before? ☐
Have you been in Toronto before? ☐

❺ Did you have a good flight? ☐
Had you a good flight? ☐

❻ Would you like something to drink? ☐
Would you want something to drink? ☐

❼ I've been looking forward to meet you. ☐
I've been looking forward to meeting you. ☐

❽ We've heard so much about you. ☐
We're hearing so much about you. ☐

❾ I'll let Mr. Song know that you arrived. ☐
I'll inform Mr. Song know you arrived. ☐

❿ Is this your first visit in India? ☐
Is this your first visit to India? ☐

◀))

⚙ 40.2 REWRITE THE SENTENCES, CORRECTING THE ERRORS

I'm eating a pasta for lunch today.
I'm eating some pasta for lunch today.

❶ Is there some information about flights?
_____

❷ I need to buy any food.
_____

❸ Are there some good hotels nearby?
_____

❹ Can I get you some cup of coffee?
_____

❺ Are there some interesting talks today?
_____

❻ Do you have some luggage?
_____

❼ There is some presentation later.
_____

❽ Do you have some tea?
_____

❾ Please take some seat at the front.
_____

◀))

40.3 MATCH THE BEGINNINGS OF THE SENTENCES TO THE CORRECT ENDINGS

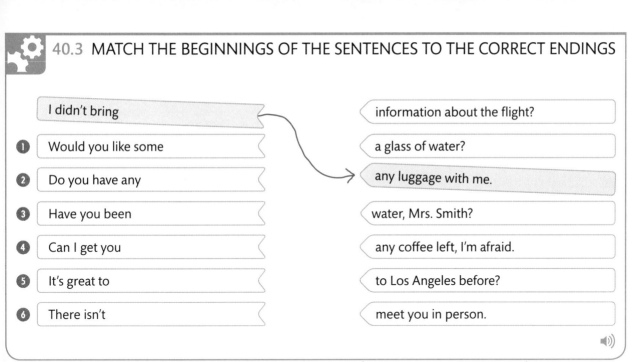

I didn't bring

1. Would you like some
2. Do you have any
3. Have you been
4. Can I get you
5. It's great to
6. There isn't

information about the flight?

a glass of water?

any luggage with me.

water, Mrs. Smith?

any coffee left, I'm afraid.

to Los Angeles before?

meet you in person.

40.4 CROSS OUT THE INCORRECT WORD IN EACH SENTENCE, THEN SAY THE SENTENCES OUT LOUD

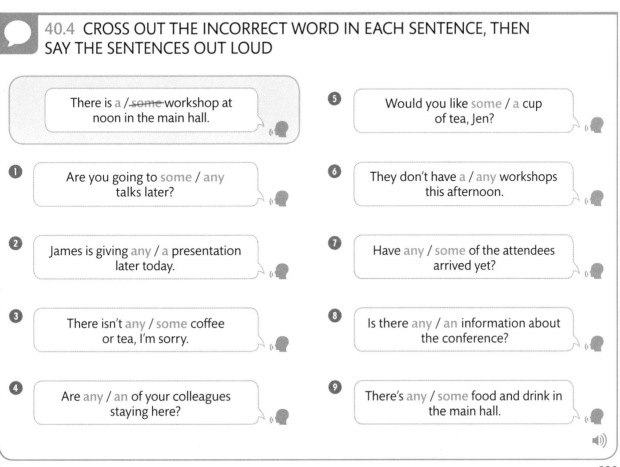

There is a / some workshop at noon in the main hall.

1. Are you going to some / any talks later?

2. James is giving any / a presentation later today.

3. There isn't any / some coffee or tea, I'm sorry.

4. Are any / an of your colleagues staying here?

5. Would you like some / a cup of tea, Jen?

6. They don't have a / any workshops this afternoon.

7. Have any / some of the attendees arrived yet?

8. Is there any / an information about the conference?

9. There's any / some food and drink in the main hall.

129

iTech99
Where the future is discussed today...

Welcome to our 15th annual iTech99 conference!
Guests should report to reception at the Lions Hotel, where they can collect their name badges and conference pack. The opening plenary will be in the main hall from 3pm to 5pm, during which our keynote speaker, Doctor Arnold Smith, CEO of AstroPlus, will discuss how to develop an effective app. In the evening, there will be a reception at the Westerton Hotel. A choice of snacks and drinks will be served.

On Tuesday, AstroPlus will launch their new phone, the GH34. This will be an excellent chance for networking, during which delegates can meet some of the big stars from the world of technology.

Wednesday will see a question-and-answer session, during which attendees will have the chance to ask the some of the CEOs from the tech giants questions.

Finally on Friday, there will be talks about new developments in marketing and changes in the Asian market.

Guests should collect their conference packs from...
their hotel. ☐   **reception.** ☑   **the main hall.** ☐

❶ The opening plenary will take place in...
the main hall. ☐   **the Westerton Hotel.** ☐   **the reception area.** ☐

❷ The keynote speaker will discuss...
his company's future. ☐   **developing an app.** ☐   **building an IT team.** ☐

❸ At the reception there will be...
live music. ☐   **a choice of food and drink.** ☐   **team-building exercises.** ☐

❹ On Tuesday, there will be...
a product launch. ☐   **a question-and-answer session.** ☐   **a final plenary.** ☐

❺ During the question-and-answer session, attendees will meet...
consumer focus groups. ☐   **leading CEOs.** ☐   **journalists.** ☐

❻ The talks on Friday will discuss...
the Asian market. ☐   **networking.** ☐   **the European market.** ☐

41 Dining and hospitality

It is important to learn local customs for dining and entertaining. At business lunches and conferences, follow these customs and use polite language.

🔧 **New language** "Much / many," "too / enough"
Aa Vocabulary Restaurants
🧩 **New skill** Offering and accepting hospitality

41.1 MARK THE BEST REPLY TO EACH QUESTION

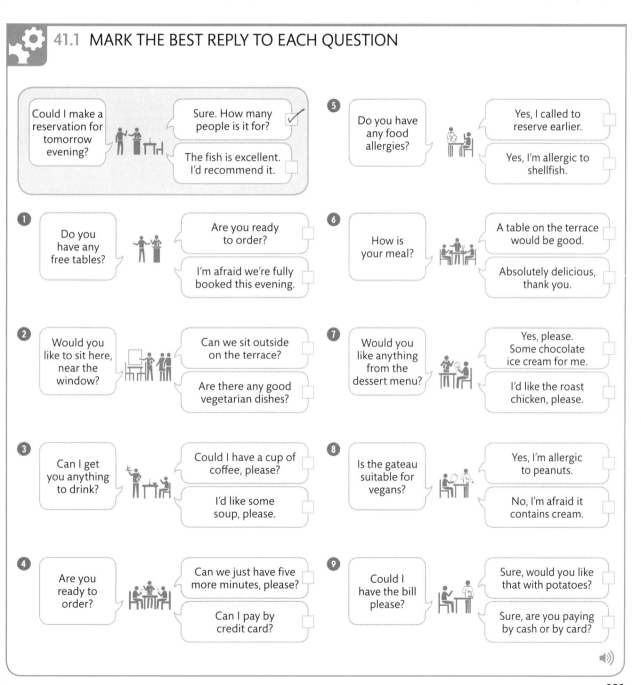

Could I make a reservation for tomorrow evening?
- Sure. How many people is it for? ✓
- The fish is excellent. I'd recommend it.

1 Do you have any free tables?
- Are you ready to order?
- I'm afraid we're fully booked this evening.

2 Would you like to sit here, near the window?
- Can we sit outside on the terrace?
- Are there any good vegetarian dishes?

3 Can I get you anything to drink?
- Could I have a cup of coffee, please?
- I'd like some soup, please.

4 Are you ready to order?
- Can we just have five more minutes, please?
- Can I pay by credit card?

5 Do you have any food allergies?
- Yes, I called to reserve earlier.
- Yes, I'm allergic to shellfish.

6 How is your meal?
- A table on the terrace would be good.
- Absolutely delicious, thank you.

7 Would you like anything from the dessert menu?
- Yes, please. Some chocolate ice cream for me.
- I'd like the roast chicken, please.

8 Is the gateau suitable for vegans?
- Yes, I'm allergic to peanuts.
- No, I'm afraid it contains cream.

9 Could I have the bill please?
- Sure, would you like that with potatoes?
- Sure, are you paying by cash or by card?

🔊

41.2 REWRITE THE SENTENCES, PUTTING THE WORDS IN THE CORRECT ORDER

a   I'm   wait.   15-minute   there's   afraid

I'm afraid there's a 15-minute wait.

❶ you   to   Are   order?   ready

_____

❷ reserve   for   like   to   please.   I'd   table   two,   a

_____

❸ reserved   madam?   Have   you   table,   a

_____

❹ people   many   there   in   party?   How   are   your

_____

❺ at   please?   dessert   I   a   the   have   menu,   Could   look

_____

❻ the   you   would   What   for   like   entree?

_____

❼ or   you   Do   any   allergies   intolerances?   have

_____

❽ many   are   How   there   today?   options   vegetarian

_____

❾ the   we   bill,   have   please?   Could

_____

❿ you   to   cash   like   card?   or   by   Would   pay

_____

41.3 MARK THE SENTENCES THAT ARE CORRECT

How much does the steak cost? ✓
How many does the steak cost? ☐

1 How many chairs will you need? ☐
How many chair will you need? ☐

2 I ordered too many dishes. ☐
I ordered enough dishes. ☐

3 There's enough space here. It's tiny. ☐
There's not enough space here. It's tiny. ☐

4 How many plates will you need? ☐
How much plates will you need? ☐

5 There are too many chairs. ☐
There are too much chairs. ☐

6 There's not many cake for everyone. ☐
There's not enough cake for everyone. ☐

7 The lobster costs too much. ☐
The lobster costs not enough. ☐

8 We haven't ordered enough dishes. ☐
We haven't ordered too many dishes. ☐

9 How much guests are you expecting? ☐
How many guests are you expecting? ☐

10 I don't have many cash for a tip. ☐
I don't have enough cash for a tip. ☐

11 I've eaten too much food this evening! ☐
I've eaten too many food this evening! ☐

12 There's enough tea for everyone. ☐
There's much tea for everyone. ☐

◀))

41.4 SAY THE SENTENCES OUT LOUD, FILLING IN THE GAPS USING THE WORDS IN THE PANEL

Tell me how _____much_____ rice you'd like. 🔊

1 How _____ people are coming tonight?

2 Is there _____ space at the table for everyone?

3 How _____ does the meal usually cost?

4 I've eaten too _____ cake.

5 There's _____ much salt in my soup.

6 There are not _____ chairs for all of us!

7 _____ many glasses will we need this evening?

How	~~much~~	too	much
enough	much	many	enough

◀))

133

42 Informal phone calls

In most workplaces, you can use polite but informal language to call your co-workers. English often uses two- or three-part verbs in informal telephone language.

⚙ **New language** Telephone language
Aa Vocabulary Phone numbers and etiquette
🧩 **New skill** Calling your co-workers

42.1 FILL IN THE GAPS USING THE WORDS IN THE PANEL

Hello. Colin _____ *speaking* _____.

1 I'd _____ go now.

2 Can I _____ who's calling?

3 No, that's _____ , thanks.

4 OK. _____ to you soon.

5 Is there _____ else I can do?

6 Hello, Sales _____.

| anything | department | Talk |
| ask | ~~speaking~~ | better | all |

🔊

42.2 LISTEN TO THE AUDIO, THEN NUMBER THE SENTENCES IN THE ORDER YOU HEAR THEM

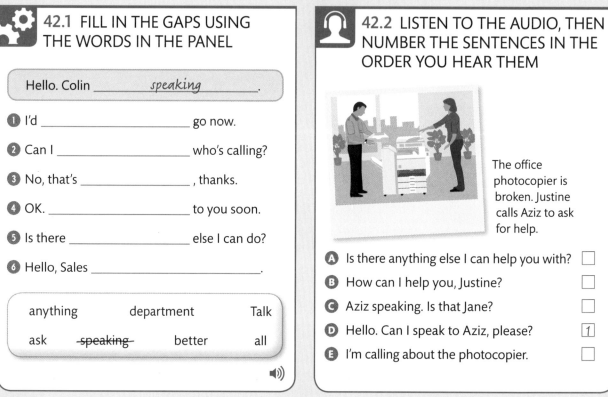

The office photocopier is broken. Justine calls Aziz to ask for help.

A Is there anything else I can help you with? ☐

B How can I help you, Justine? ☐

C Aziz speaking. Is that Jane? ☐

D Hello. Can I speak to Aziz, please? 1

E I'm calling about the photocopier. ☐

42.3 MATCH THE SENTENCES WITH THE CORRECT RESPONSES

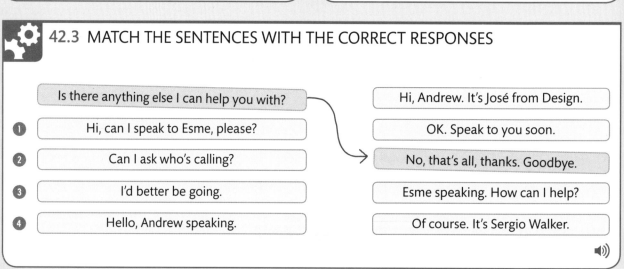

Is there anything else I can help you with?

1 Hi, can I speak to Esme, please?

2 Can I ask who's calling?

3 I'd better be going.

4 Hello, Andrew speaking.

Hi, Andrew. It's José from Design.

OK. Speak to you soon.

No, that's all, thanks. Goodbye.

Esme speaking. How can I help?

Of course. It's Sergio Walker.

🔊

42.4 LISTEN TO THE AUDIO AND WRITE DOWN THE TELEPHONE NUMBERS THAT YOU HEAR

0 7 3 5 8 1 3 5 2 8 8

4 _____

1 _____

5 _____

2 _____

6 _____

3 _____

7 _____

42.5 LOOK AT THE BUSINESS CARDS, THEN RESPOND TO THE AUDIO, SPEAKING OUT LOUD

What is Ben's office number?

Ben's office number is 01928 335570.

1 What's Liz's extension?

2 What's Saira's office number?

3 What's the Helpdesk number at KTV News?

4 What's Lucy's cell phone number?

Bettina's fashions

ACCOUNTS DIRECTOR: Ben Tibbs
Tel.: 01928 335570 · Ext.: 5570
Cell phone: 07327 559801

DIRECTOR'S PA: Liz Banks
Tel: 01928 333864 · Ext.: 3864

ACCOUNTANT: Saira Dhabi
Tel.: 01928 335178 · Ext.: 5178
Cell phone: 07932 358916

K TV NEWS

IT 24/7 HELPDESK:
Tel.: (616) 888-3746

DIGITAL DIRECTOR: Lucy Kehoe
Tel: (616) 885-5392 · Ext.: 8539
Cell phone: (616) 913-6205

PROGRAMMER: Sami Patel
Cell phone: (616) 561-0324

42.6 FILL IN THE GAPS USING THE PHRASES IN THE PANEL

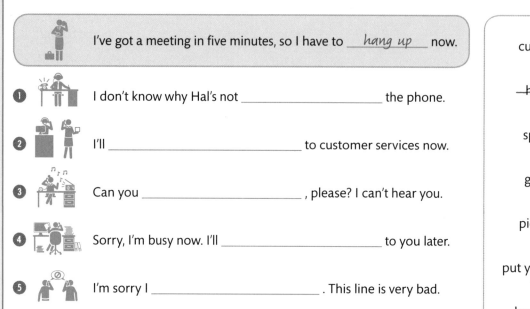

I've got a meeting in five minutes, so I have to ___hang up___ now.

1 I don't know why Hal's not _____ the phone.

2 I'll _____ to customer services now.

3 Can you _____ , please? I can't hear you.

4 Sorry, I'm busy now. I'll _____ to you later.

5 I'm sorry I _____ . This line is very bad.

6 You're _____ . Can I call you back?

Panel:
- cut you off
- ~~hang up~~
- speak up
- get back
- picking up
- put you through
- breaking up

42.7 CROSS OUT THE INCORRECT WORDS IN EACH SENTENCE

Don't hang ~~on~~ / ~~down~~ / up. I need to talk to you about the China sales.

1 Could you possibly speak on / off / up, please? The line is very faint.

2 I'll call they / you / us back in ten minutes. Is that OK? I have to finish writing an email.

3 If I get cut of / on / off, call me back on the office phone. I'm back at my desk now.

4 Can I get back to / with / from you about the design later today? We're still working on it.

5 I've called Fatima three times, but she didn't pick on / up / over. Is she at work today?

6 Marc kept breaking for / up / down when I called him. The signal here is awful!

7 Katie is back at her desk now. I'll just put you through / over / up to her.

8 Mateo got back for / to / of me about the new manual. He has a few comments on it.

| hang | rude | can | on | You | customer. | up | a |

You can hang up on a rude customer.

1 you | please? | speak | Can | up,

_____

2 get | hope | off | cut | I | again. | don't | I

_____

3 me | Let | Finance. | through | put | to | you

_____

4 you | I | pick | up | didn't | called. | Sorry | when

_____

5 back | him | you | afternoon? | to | get | this | Can

_____

6 the | breaking | keeps | Sorry, | up. | line

_____

7 five | I'll | you | minutes. | call | back | in

_____

8 yesterday. | He | back | to | didn't | get | me

_____

9 up | Don't | Dan | pick | the | calls. | phone | if

_____

◀))

137

43 Formal phone calls

When you talk to clients or receptionists, you may
need to use formal language on the phone. You
may also need to take or leave a phone message.

⚙ **New language** Adjective order
Aa **Vocabulary** Formal telephone language
🧩 **New skill** Leaving phone messages

43.1 MARK THE BEST REPLY TO EACH STATEMENT

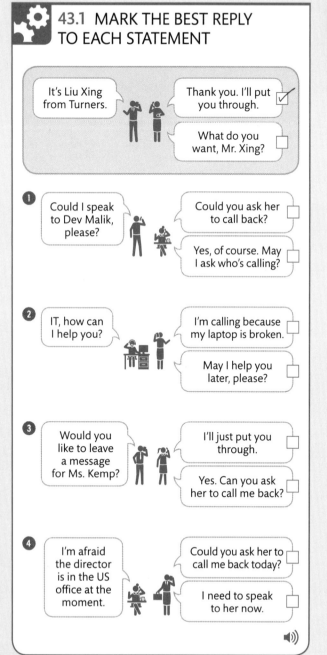

It's Liu Xing from Turners.

Thank you. I'll put you through. ✓

What do you want, Mr. Xing? ☐

1. Could I speak to Dev Malik, please?

Could you ask her to call back? ☐

Yes, of course. May I ask who's calling? ☐

2. IT, how can I help you?

I'm calling because my laptop is broken. ☐

May I help you later, please? ☐

3. Would you like to leave a message for Ms. Kemp?

I'll just put you through. ☐

Yes. Can you ask her to call me back? ☐

4. I'm afraid the director is in the US office at the moment.

Could you ask her to call me back today? ☐

I need to speak to her now. ☐

🔊

43.2 CROSS OUT THE INCORRECT WORD IN EACH SENTENCE, THEN SAY THE SENTENCES OUT LOUD

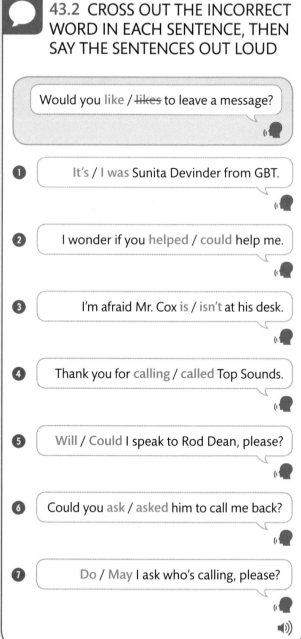

Would you like / ~~likes~~ to leave a message?

1. It's / I was Sunita Devinder from GBT.

2. I wonder if you helped / could help me.

3. I'm afraid Mr. Cox is / isn't at his desk.

4. Thank you for calling / called Top Sounds.

5. Will / Could I speak to Rod Dean, please?

6. Could you ask / asked him to call me back?

7. Do / May I ask who's calling, please?

🔊

43.3 MARK THE SENTENCES THAT ARE CORRECT

I'm afraid my manager isn't here. ☑
I'm apologize my manager isn't here. ☐

1 How can I helps you? ☐
How can I help you? ☐

2 May I ask who's calling? ☐
May I ask who calls? ☐

3 I'll yet put you through. ☐
I'll just put you through. ☐

4 Will you like to leave a message? ☐
Would you like to leave a message? ☐

5 Could you ask him to call me back, please? ☐
Could you ask him call me back, please? ☐

6 How can I help you? IT department. ☐
IT department. How can I help you? ☐

7 I'll put you over to HR now. ☐
I'll put you through to HR now. ☐

8 I'm afraid he's not on his desk. ☐
I'm afraid he's not at his desk. ☐

9 Thank you for calling Quadfax. ☐
Thank you to call Quadfax. ☐

◀))

43.4 FILL IN THE GAPS USING THE PHRASES IN THE PANEL

Yes, of course. _____May I ask_____ who's calling?

1 Savino's. How _____ you?

2 Thank you _____ Ready Solutions.

3 Hello. _____ you can help me.

4 I'm calling _____ I placed last month.

5 _____ to Becky Bradley, please?

6 I'm afraid the Accounts Manager is away _____.

7 Yes, please. _____ 20 desks?

8 _____ to leave a message?

9 Thank you. _____ you through.

I'll just put

Could I speak

can I help

~~May I ask~~

Would you like

about an order

Could I order

at the moment

for calling

I wonder if

◀))

139

Aa 43.5 WRITE THE WORDS FROM THE PANEL IN THE CORRECT GROUPS

OPINION	SIZE	AGE	COLOR	MATERIAL
nice				

ancient   blue   leather   awful   tiny   ~~nice~~   metal   modern

purple   stylish   pink   large   plastic   antique   huge

43.6 REWRITE THE SENTENCES, PUTTING THE WORDS IN THE CORRECT ORDER

beautiful   laptop   new   is   model.   a   My   silver

My laptop is a beautiful new silver model.

1. little   gold   lamp.   We're   a   stylish   developing

2. amazing   new   has   Tom   tiny   an   smartphone.   got

3. a   has   cat.   black and white   pet store   big   The   nice

4. in   is   large   There   an   painting   awful   cafeteria.   modern   the

5. exciting   seen   the   marketing   Have   posters?   new   you   colorful

43.7 MATCH THE PICTURES TO THE CORRECT SENTENCES

That's a stylish new design for the company logo.

1 Eco Fashion

Let's have lunch at that nice big café in the square.

2

There's a big yellow and red truck outside.

3

There's a nice big green and white plant in my office.

4

There's a huge round hole in the wall where the truck hit it.

5

Have you seen the fabulous new office chairs?

6

Have you tasted the awful new coffee?

7

There's a large rectangular parking space for motorbikes.

8

The headphones for my laptop go in a tiny round hole.

🔊

43.8 LISTEN TO THE AUDIO AND ANSWER THE QUESTIONS

 Shaun calls a hotel to make arrangements for a conference.

Who does Shaun want to speak to?
The receptionist ☐
The hotel manager ☑
The customer services department ☐

1 What does Shaun's company produce?
Sports cars ☐
Printed materials ☐
Cakes and cookies ☐

2 When is the conference?
Next Monday ☐
Next Thursday ☐
Next Tuesday ☐

3 What time will the conference start?
9:00 ☐
9:30 ☐
9:00–9:30 ☐

4 How many attendees will there be?
50 ☐
56 ☐
60 ☐

5 What else does Shaun ask to book?
Six taxis ☐
A minibus ☐
An extra meeting room ☐

6 What extra dietary requests does Shaun make?
Vegetarian and vegan food ☐
Vegan and gluten-free food ☐
Vegetarian and gluten-free food ☐

44 Writing a résumé

A résumé (or CV in UK English) is a clear summary of your skills and career history. Past simple action verbs are particularly useful for describing past achievements.

☼ **New language** Action verbs for achievements
Aa Vocabulary Résumé vocabulary
New skill Writing a résumé

Aa 44.1 MATCH THE DEFINITIONS TO THE CORRECT RÉSUMÉ HEADINGS

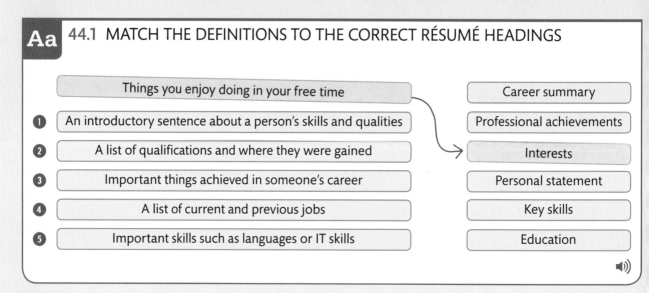

Things you enjoy doing in your free time

1 An introductory sentence about a person's skills and qualities

2 A list of qualifications and where they were gained

3 Important things achieved in someone's career

4 A list of current and previous jobs

5 Important skills such as languages or IT skills

Career summary

Professional achievements

Interests

Personal statement

Key skills

Education

44.2 REWRITE THE SENTENCES, CORRECTING THE ERRORS

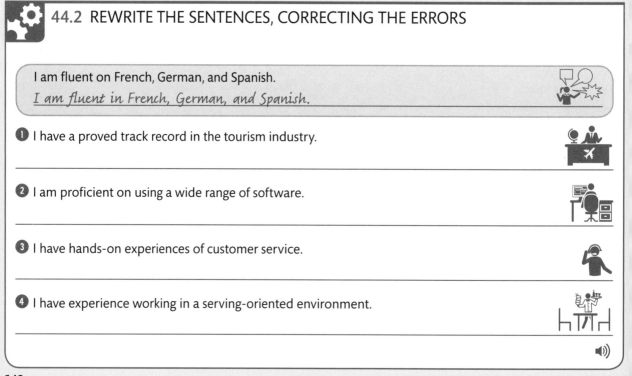

I am fluent on French, German, and Spanish.
I am fluent in French, German, and Spanish.

1 I have a proved track record in the tourism industry.

2 I am proficient on using a wide range of software.

3 I have hands-on experiences of customer service.

4 I have experience working in a serving-oriented environment.

44.3 REWRITE THE SENTENCES, PUTTING THE WORDS IN THE CORRECT ORDER

and | in | French, | I | am | German, | English. | fluent

I am fluent in French, German, and English.

1 in | individual | working | am | motivated | and | highly | love | I | tourism. | a

_____

2 construction | I | knowledge | the | gained | of | industry. | in-depth

_____

3 in | experience | catering | I | a | of | the | great | deal | industry. | have

_____

4 software. | am | in | most | types | I | accounting | of | proficient

_____

◀))

44.4 CROSS OUT THE INCORRECT WORD IN EACH SENTENCE

 I volunteered / ~~collaborated~~ for a local charity.

1 I managed / negotiated a large team of marketing executives.

2 Our teams collaborated / co-ordinated to create a new clothing range.

3 The company established / volunteered a new headquarters in the capital.

4 I collaborated / negotiated with our suppliers and got a good deal.

44.5 READ THE RÉSUMÉ AND WRITE ANSWERS TO THE QUESTIONS AS FULL SENTENCES

AYIDA LAMIA

123 Hills Road
Cambridge, MA 02138
ayida@lamia.com (617) 548-81313

PERSONAL STATEMENT
I am a highly motivated individual who enjoys working with others to creatively problem solve. I have a proven track record in the field of accounting.

PROFESSIONAL ACHIEVEMENTS
I oversaw the introduction of new accounting software and co-ordinated a training program for all staff in Accounts last year.

WORK EXPERIENCE
Tomkins Travel
Deputy Director of Accounts April 2013 – present
• I oversee the processing and auditing of the company's accounts
• I train staff to use a range of software packages

Kelsey Homes
Accountant September 2010 – April 2013
• I was responsible for the accounts of a construction company building new homes.

EDUCATION
• Diploma in Accounting June 2010
• BA in Business June 2009

KEY SKILLS
• Proficient in IT use, including all major accountancy software
• Fluent in Spanish and English, intermediate level Polish
• First aid qualified; I am a named first aider in the workplace

INTERESTS
Acting in the local drama group, traveling, and reading contemporary fiction

References available upon request.

How does Ayida describe herself in her personal statement?

She says she is highly motivated.

❶ What does Ayida count as a notable professional achievement?

_____

❷ What is Ayida's current job?

_____

❸ What industry did Ayida work in before her current role?

_____

❹ When did Ayida gain her diploma in Accounting?

_____

❺ What languages can Ayida speak fluently?

_____

45 Making plans

English uses the future with "going to" to talk about plans and decisions that have already been made. It is useful for informing co-workers about your plans.

New language The future with "going to"
Aa Vocabulary Polite requests
New skill Making arrangements and plans

45.1 FILL IN THE GAPS USING THE FUTURE WITH "GOING TO"

I _____am going to call_____ (call) the Miami office this afternoon.

1. He _____ (travel) to the conference by plane.

2. She _____ (not make) it to the meeting.

3. They _____ (meet) the staff from the Paris office.

4. He _____ (write) a letter to the suppliers.

5. They _____ (not sell) their shares in the company just now.

6. _____ she _____ (order) business cards with the new company logo?

7. Sergio _____ (give) a presentation about the new training course.

8. _____ you _____ (make) tea and coffee for the visitors?

9. Diana _____ (design) the new company logo.

10. They _____ (join) us for our team meeting today.

11. _____ you _____ (review) the sales data this afternoon?

45.2 MARK THE MOST POLITE SENTENCE OF EACH PAIR

Please could you call a taxi? ✓
You have to call a taxi now. ☐

1 Why don't we ask what Marketing think? ☐
I want to ask Marketing what they think. ☐

2 Load the printer with paper. ☐
Could you load the printer with paper? ☐

3 Can you help me with these files, please? ☐
I need help with these files. ☐

4 You should send the files to production. ☐
Could you send the files to production? ☐

5 Could we meet at 4 instead of 5? ☐
I want to meet at 4 instead of 5. ☐

6 Can you finish the report today? ☐
Why haven't you finished the report? ☐

7 We need to invite Jeff to the meeting. ☐
Couldn't we invite Jeff to the meeting? ☐

8 Could you call me back later, please? ☐
I'm too busy to talk to you now. ☐

9 Could you make coffee for the CEO? ☐
You have to make coffee for the CEO. ☐

10 We need to cancel the meeting. ☐
Could we possibly cancel the meeting? ☐

11 You must check this report. ☐
Can you check this report, please? ☐

12 Could you pass round the agenda? ☐
Pass round the agenda. ☐

13 Can we try a different approach? ☐
Your approach to this isn't working. ☐

14 You must call the Delhi office now. ☐
Please could you call the Delhi office? ☐

15 Could you lock up before you leave? ☐
Why haven't you locked the door? ☐

16 Could you possibly stay late tonight? ☐
You have to stay late tonight. ☐

17 Have you printed out these designs? ☐
Please can you print out these designs? ☐

◀))

45.3 USE THE CHART TO CREATE 18 CORRECT SENTENCES AND SAY THEM OUT LOUD

I am going to email the director.

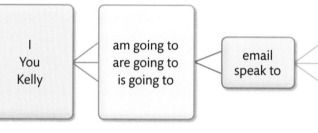

| I / You / Kelly | am going to / are going to / is going to | email / speak to | the director. / the IT help desk. / the sales department. |

◀))

45.4 LISTEN TO THE AUDIO AND ANSWER THE QUESTIONS

Diego and Janet are organizing a conference.

Diego is going to call the hotel.
True ✓ **False** ☐ **Not given** ☐

❶ The Boston office will attend the conference.
True ☐ **False** ☐ **Not given** ☐

❷ Diego doesn't like the company logo designs.
True ☐ **False** ☐ **Not given** ☐

❸ Janet is going to make the name badges.
True ☐ **False** ☐ **Not given** ☐

❹ Diego is going to check that the rooms have Wi-Fi.
True ☐ **False** ☐ **Not given** ☐

❺ The interns won't be involved in the conference.
True ☐ **False** ☐ **Not given** ☐

45.5 READ THE EMAIL AND WRITE ANSWERS TO THE QUESTIONS AS FULL SENTENCES

When did Jack meet Omar?

Jack met Omar on Monday.

❶ Who is going to contact the presenters?

_____

❷ What is Paul going to ask the printers for?

_____

❸ What else are the printers going to supply?

_____

❹ Who is going to meet the presenters?

_____

❺ How will the presenters get to the venue?

_____

❻ Why is Omar going to go to the venue?

_____

✉ ⌄ ✕

To: Jack Brown

Subject: Training day preparations

Hi Jack,
Following our meeting on Monday, I have an update on the preparations for the training day. I spoke to Paul and he is going to contact the presenters. He's also going to call the printers and ask if they can print ten extra copies of the training booklets. We have asked the printers to supply name badges in the form of lanyards. They are going to assemble the name badges to save us time.

Marie is going to meet the presenters at the station and bring them to the conference center by taxi. I am going to the venue later today to talk to the catering manager. We have quite a few delegates with special dietary requirements so I want to check they will be catered for. I'll email you later with a further update.
Best wishes,
Omar

46 Vocabulary

46.1 FORMS OF COMMUNICATION WRITE THE WORDS FROM THE PANEL UNDER THE CORRECT PICTURES

switchboard

1 _____

2 _____

3 _____

4 _____

5 _____

6 _____

7 _____

8 _____

9 _____

10 _____

11 _____

12 _____

13 _____

14 _____

15 _____

envelope   text message   social networking   voicemail   ~~switchboard~~   stamp

bulletin board (US) / notice board (UK)   transfer a call   conference call   internal mail

web conference   mail (US) / post (UK)   presentation   letter   website   email

Aa 46.2 SENDING EMAILS WRITE THE WORDS FROM THE PANEL UNDER THE CORRECT PICTURES

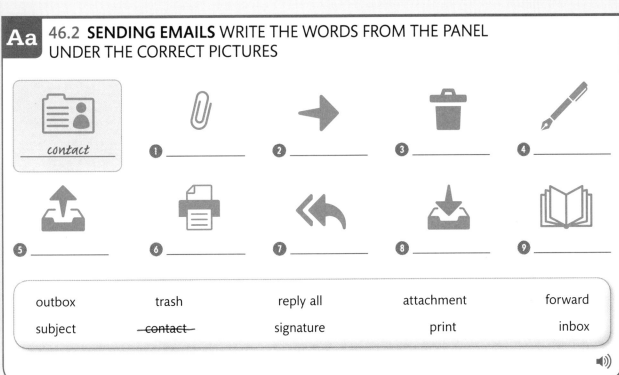

contact

1 _____

2 _____

3 _____

4 _____

5 _____

6 _____

7 _____

8 _____

9 _____

outbox   trash   reply all   attachment   forward

subject   ~~contact~~   signature   print   inbox

Aa 46.3 ABBREVIATIONS WRITE THE ABBREVIATIONS FROM THE PANEL UNDER THE CORRECT DEFINITIONS

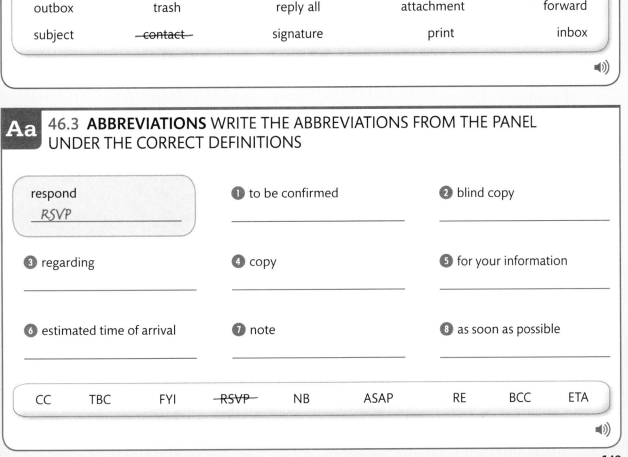

respond
RSVP

1 to be confirmed
_____

2 blind copy
_____

3 regarding
_____

4 copy
_____

5 for your information
_____

6 estimated time of arrival
_____

7 note
_____

8 as soon as possible
_____

CC   TBC   FYI   ~~RSVP~~   NB   ASAP   RE   BCC   ETA

47 Emailing a client

Emails to clients should be polite and clearly state your future plans and intentions. Use the present continuous or "going to" to discuss plans and arrangements.

🔧 **New language** Future tenses for plans
Aa Vocabulary Polite email language
🧩 **New skill** Emailing a client

 47.1 REWRITE THE SENTENCES, CORRECTING THE ERRORS

> I am writing with regarding to your order.
> *I am writing with regard to your order.*

1 I work at the finance department at Forrester's.

2 Please confirm your availability APAS.

3 Please find your attached receipt to this email.

4 Please hesitate not to contact me.

5 I am writing reference with invoice number 146.

6 Please see the agenda attach here.

7 I work in the IT department in Transtech.

8 I writing to invite you to a meeting next week.

9 Please hesitate to contact me.

10 Please return ASAP your signed contract.

11 I be grateful if you could get back to me soon.

12 I am writing regard to your complaint.

13 Please find the minutes attachment here.

14 I would grateful if we could arrange a meeting.

15 I work at the company's catering department.

16 I am the new Head of Sales in Codequote.

17 I am writing with regard our schedule.

18 Please let me know if you any questions.

19 Please finding the new designs attached here.

🔊

47.2 REWRITE THE SENTENCES, PUTTING THE WORDS IN THE CORRECT ORDER

would · if · ASAP. · grateful · could · you · I · be · me · contact

I would be grateful if you could contact me ASAP.

❶ to · your · writing · latest · regard · I · feedback. · am · with

_____

❷ invoice · here. · the · Please · attached · find

_____

❸ grateful · would · invoice. · if · pay · could · the · I · outstanding · be · you

_____

❹ do · questions, · If · contact · any · me. · please · not · you · to · have · hesitate

_____

🔊

47.3 MATCH THE BEGINNINGS OF THE SENTENCES TO THE CORRECT ENDINGS

If you have any questions,	could let us know when you have been paid.
❶ I am writing with	that invoice DY895 has not been paid.
❷ I work in	please do not hesitate to contact me.
❸ I would be grateful if you	the supply and payment of invoices.
❹ I deal with	you are aware that we have not been paid.
❺ It has come to our attention	the accounts department at Shuberg's.
❻ I wonder if	inform you that we are going to use a new supplier.
❼ I am writing to	regard to our invoice number AB3168.

🔊

We're _____*going to send*_____ you the package you ordered ASAP.

① He _____ all the candidates a task to do before their interview.

② We _____ other suppliers on Tuesday.

③ Sam _____ coffee for the CEO's visitors.

④ Carlos _____ the sales figures tomorrow.

⑤ We _____ sales figures for the last quarter.

⑥ They _____ all their clients a voucher.

⑦ He _____ to Italy to meet the new CEO.

⑧ Greg _____ all the boxes into the delivery van.

⑨ A famous hairdresser _____ the new salon.

⑩ We _____ the new company logo at the sales conference.

⑪ The company _____ all the stationery with the old logo.

---

is going to pack   is giving   is going to make   is going to recycle

      are going to discuss   are meeting   ~~going to send~~   are launching

is going to travel   is presenting   are giving   is going to open

---

152

47.5 MARK THE SENTENCES THAT ARE CORRECT

I am writing to inform you that we paying your invoice ASAP. ☐
I am writing to inform you that we are going to pay your invoice ASAP. ☑

1 I am writing with regard to the shareholders' meeting on Thursday. ☐
I am writing with regarding the shareholders' meeting on Thursday. ☐

2 We are going to meeting new clients at the Radcliffe Hotel. ☐
We are meeting new clients at the Radcliffe Hotel. ☐

3 The meeting is taking place in the hotel's conference center. ☐
The meeting is going take place in the hotel's conference center. ☐

4 We is going to discuss the last quarter's sales figures. ☐
We are going to discuss the last quarter's sales figures. ☐

5 The new CEO is go to take questions after his presentation. ☐
The new CEO is taking questions after his presentation. ☐

6 He is going to discuss the company's future marketing strategy. ☐
He is going to discussing the company's future marketing strategy. ☐

◀))

47.6 READ THE EMAIL AND MARK THE CORRECT SUMMARY

1 Bruno wants to meet the Head of Marketing but cannot find a suitable time. ☐

2 Bruno suggests that Ms. Moran should contact the Head of Marketing directly. ☐

3 Bruno wants to arrange a meeting. His client has not yet confirmed a suitable time for it. ☐

4 Bruno wants to arrange a conference for Mr. Jefferies. ☐

✉ ⌄ ✕

To: Laila Moran

Subject: Date for meeting

Dear Ms. Moran,
I work in the marketing department of Hailey's. I am writing with regard to the meeting you wish to have with our Head of Marketing about the launch of your new products. As you will recall, I wrote to you a week ago asking when you would be available to meet at our premises. Mr. Jefferies has availability next Wednesday afternoon and also on the morning of Friday, July 14. If you could confirm which of those slots works for you, I would be most grateful. I will then send you all the documentation ahead of your meeting with Mr. Jefferies.
Kind regards,
Bruno Martell

↩ ↩↩   📎 🗑

Answers

01

1.1 🔊
1. My name's Ali Patel.
2. Hi, I'm Jeff.
3. It's good to meet you, Jane.
4. Pleased to meet you.
5. My name is Deepak Kaur.
6. Great to meet you, Tanya.
7. It's nice to meet you, too.
8. Good morning. My name is Ben Lewis.
9. It's great to meet you, Gill.
10. Good evening. My name is Karen.

1.2 🔊
1. Hello, my name's Fiona Hill.
2. Nice to meet you, too.
3. It's good to meet you, Jim.
4. Pleased to meet you.
5. It's a pleasure to meet you.
6. Good evening. My name is Roy.

1.3
1. A
2. B
3. B
4. A
5. A

1.4 🔊
1. A-L-E-X H-A-N-N
2. D-E-V S-I-N-G-H
3. F-R-A-N-C-I-S P-A-L-M-E-R
4. H-A-N-S-A S-Y-A
5. Z-A-N-D-R-A F-E-L-L-I-N-I
6. R-A-J D-H-A-B-I
7. K-A-T-Y A-D-E-N-O-V-A

1.5 🔊
1. This **is** our new designer.
2. Raj and I **work** together.
3. I **would** like you to meet our CEO. / **I'd** like you to meet our CEO.
4. Hi, **my** name's Lola. / Hi, **I'm Lola**.

(1.5 continued)
5. It's great to **meet you**, Emily.
6. **May I** introduce Ewan Carlton?
7. Farah, this **is** my colleague, Leon.

1.6 🔊
1. Good morning. **My** name's Saira Khan.
2. **I'm** Harry.
3. **I'm** Andrew Shaw.
4. **It's** good to meet you.
5. Pleased **to** meet you.
6. It's a **pleasure** to meet you.
7. **May** I introduce our new HR assistant?
8. Keira, **meet** John.
9. **Great** to meet you.
10. I **would** like you to meet Dan.
11. Colin and I **work** together.

1.7
A. 5
B. 6
C. 7
D. 4
E. 1
F. 3
G. 2

02

2.1 🔊
1. I start work at 9 o'clock.
2. She has an update with her boss.
3. Mrs. Reece is a fantastic teacher.
4. I'm a firefighter.
5. Elena works late on Thursdays.
6. He drinks coffee every afternoon.
7. She leaves work at 5:30pm.

2.2 🔊
1. The IT Helpdesk **is** really good.
2. She **works** in a car factory.
3. I **eat** my lunch in the park.
4. We **take** a break at 11am.
5. John **writes** the minutes of our meetings.
6. Mrs. Rae **cleans** the meeting rooms.

(2.2 continued)
7. The CEO **brings** cake on his birthday.
8. I **prepare** presentations.
9. Jomir **stops** for tea at 3pm.

2.3 🔊
1. The CEO arrives at work early.
2. We have a hot-desking policy.
3. My assistant opens my mail.
4. Shazia is an engineer.
5. Hal works for his uncle.
6. I start work at 8:30am.
7. They finish at 5pm.
8. They eat lunch in the cafeteria.
9. Kate only drinks coffee.
10. I call the US office every Monday.
11. Andrew helps me with my PC.
12. I reply to emails at 11am and 3pm.

2.4
1. The manager's PA
2. After the break
3. An hour
4. 12:30pm
5. They analyze sales
6. Twice a week

2.5 🔊
1. The director **has** an open door policy.
2. I **deal** with all his emails.
3. Gavin **leaves** work at 7pm.
4. They **work** evenings and weekends.
5. She **rides** her bike to work.
6. Tim and Pat **bring** their own lunch.
7. Deepak **turns** off his phone after work.
8. Sobek and Kurt **play** tennis after work.
9. My boss **plans** my work for the week.

2.6 🔊
1. Lulu always **gets** to work early.
2. Our reps **meet** clients at their office.
3. The CEO **talks** to all new staff.
4. He's a nurse and he **works** weekends.
5. Imran **deals** with all the contracts.
6. The printer **stops** working late in the day.
7. The staff **go** to a nearby café for lunch.
8. Raj **takes** a break at 11am.
9. Sophie **is** a travel agent.

03

3.1 🔊
1. Argentina
2. Australia
3. South America
4. China
5. Canada
6. Egypt
7. South Korea
8. France
9. Australasia
10. Japan
11. India
12. United States of America (US / USA)
13. Netherlands
14. Asia
15. Mongolia
16. Pakistan
17. New Zealand
18. Russia
19. South Africa
20. North America
21. Thailand
22. United Arab Emirates (UAE)
23. United Kingdom (UK)
24. Turkey
25. Spain
26. Africa
27. Singapore
28. Republic of Ireland (ROI)
29. Europe
30. Mexico
31. Brazil
32. Germany
33. Austria
34. Switzerland

04

4.1
1. Russia 2. India 3. Japan
4. Chile 5. Greece

4.2
COUNTRIES:
South Africa, **France**, **Italy**, **Vietnam**, **Switzerland**, **China**
NATIONALITIES:
Brazilian, **British**, **Greek**, **Canadian**, **Japanese**, **Spanish**

4.3 🔊
1. The new CEO is **from Australia**.
2. These new robots are **Japanese**.
3. We sell leather bags **from Portugal**.
4. I'm **from Argentina**, but I work in the US.
5. The designer is **British**.
6. Our sales director is **from South Korea**.
7. Our best-selling rugs are **Indian**.
8. These beautiful clothes are **from Africa**.

4.4 🔊
1. Our CEO is from America.
2. I've got a flight to Italy next Monday.
3. These sports cars are from France.
4. Most of our fabrics are from Africa.
5. My PA is from Spain.

4.5 🔊
1. We sell smartphones from **Japan**.
2. The HR manager is from **America**.
3. My team follows the **Chinese** markets.
4. Travel to the **Greek** islands with us.
5. Our products are from **Vietnam**.
6. Our CEO is **Canadian**.
7. Most of the sales team is from **Spain**.
8. I'm British, but I work in **Italy**.
9. I have a lot of **Mexican** co-workers.
10. My new assistant is from **France**.

4.6 🔊
1. **I'm not** very tall.
2. He **doesn't work** in an office.
3. We **don't sell** French cars.
4. **They're not** from Italy. / They **aren't** from Italy.
5. The fruit in the supermarket **isn't** local.
6. I **don't work** for an Asian company.
7. **You're** not happy. / You **aren't** happy.

8. She **isn't** from China. / **She's not** from China.
9. We **don't produce** robots.
10. You **don't** have any meetings today.
11. It **isn't** a steel factory. / **It's not** a steel factory.

4.7 🔊
1. These dresses **aren't** made in India.
2. She **doesn't** come from Russia.
3. The workers in this factory **aren't** American.
4. They **don't** sell energy to South Korea.
5. He **isn't** from Chile. / **He's not** from Chile.

4.8
1. IT
2. Carlos
3. Marketing
4. Tim
5. China

4.9
1. True
2. Not given
3. False
4. True
5. Not given
6. False
7. False

05

5.1 🔊
1. adhesive tape
2. calendar
3. clipboard
4. computer
5. planner (US) / diary (UK)
6. rubber bands
7. envelope
8. hole punch
9. hard drive
10. pen
11. laptop

12 pencil
13 files / folders
14 paper clips
15 eraser (US) / rubber (UK)
16 letter
17 shredder
18 cell phone (US) / mobile phone (UK)
19 printer
20 headset
21 highlighter
22 pencil sharpener
23 stapler
24 telephone / phone
25 tablet
26 notepad
27 projector
28 chair
29 ruler
30 scanner
31 lamp

06

6.1 ◀))
1 Is this printer working?
2 Is this your desk?
3 Are the windows closed?
4 Is this cupboard locked?
5 Is his desk messy?
6 Is she the CEO?
7 Are you Jo's assistant?

6.2 ◀))
1 Is that John's pen?
2 Is this the kitchen?
3 Is that the CEO's office?
4 Is Tina the CEO's PA?
5 Is Tom's desk organized?
6 Is the printer working?
7 Is the stationery cabinet locked?

6.3 ◀))
1 **Do** you have an appointment?
2 **Does** she work with Justin?
3 **Does** your office have a scanner?
4 **Do** you go to the finance meetings?

5 **Does** Kish write the minutes?
6 **Do** you have a stapler I can borrow?
7 **Does** Saul work in your team?
8 **Do** they know what to do?
9 **Does** he know the CEO?
10 **Do** we have a meeting now?

6.4
1 False
2 True
3 False
4 False

6.5 ◀))
1 Is the stationery cabinet open?
2 Do you want tea or coffee?
3 Do you know her phone number?
4 Are they free for a meeting tomorrow?
5 Do you have a laptop I can take home?
6 Do you have an appointment?
7 Are there any envelopes I can use?
8 Does he usually arrive late?

6.6 ◀))
1 **How** does the scanner work?
2 **What** is on the agenda for the meeting?
3 **Why** is the stationery cabinet locked?
4 **When** do we have a break for lunch?
5 **Where** is the CEO's office?
6 **What** is the door code?
7 **Who** do I ask for ink for the printer?

6.7 ◀))
1 Why is the cafeteria closed?
2 How do I scan this document?
3 When is the fire alarm tested?
4 Do you know where Faisal is?
5 Is Sandra late again?
6 What is for lunch today?
7 Does the office stay open on weekends?
8 Who do you report to?

6.8 ◀))
1 **Who** buys the tea and coffee?
2 **Why** is the printer not working?
3 **When** does the office open?

4 **What** do you want for lunch?
5 **Where** is the meeting room?
6 **How** does the projector work?
7 **What** is the photocopier code?

07

7.1 ◀))
1 How can I reach you?
2 Do you have many clients?
3 Do you have a website?
4 Where do you work?
5 What is your company called?
6 What's your job title?
7 This is my email address.
8 Drop me a line.
9 How can I contact you?
10 Give me a call.
11 How big is your team?

7.2
A 6
B 2
C 3
D 5
E 1
F 4

7.3 ◀))
1 How can I **reach** you for more infomation?
2 Drop me a **line** when you're visiting next.
3 Does your company **have** a website?
4 Please stay in **touch**.
5 Is this your **correct** phone number?
6 **Call** me if you want further details.
7 Is this your **current** email address?
8 My job **title** is on the business card.
9 Do you **have** a portfolio with you?

7.4
1 True
2 True
3 Not given
4 Not given

5 False
6 True
7 False
8 False

7.5 ◄))
1 Yes, it is.
2 No, it doesn't.
3 No, they aren't.
4 Yes, I am.
5 No, he doesn't.
6 Yes, we do.

7.6 ◄))
1 No, **it isn't**.
2 No, **it doesn't**.
3 Yes, **it is**.
4 Yes, **it does**.
5 No, **they don't**.
6 No, **I'm not**.
7 Yes, **they do**.
8 Yes, **she does**.
9 Yes, **I do**.

08

8.1 ◄))
1 She **has** an excellent résumé.
2 I **have** good people skills.
3 They **don't have** much time.
4 Do you **have** previous experience?
5 He's **got** excellent keyboard skills.
6 I **don't have** my own office.
7 Does he **have** any training?
8 They **have** a can-do outlook.
9 You don't **have** his number, do you?

8.2 ◄))
1 Do you have a higher degree in business?
2 He has an MBA from the Boston Business School.
3 They don't have a full-time receptionist.
4 Does your assistant have an excellent résumé?

8.3
1 Travel
2 A hotel
3 Management
4 Excellent
5 In teams
6 Marketing

8.4 ◄))
1 The new chef is very talented.
2 Toby is an accountant.
3 Search engines are invaluable.
4 She works for a leading company.
5 Have you seen the ad I told you about?
6 They are out of the office.
7 Did you see the new designs?
8 They hired the best candidate.
9 What skills does the job require?
10 Is there an office in India?
11 I have a certificate in sales.
12 He works for the biggest store.
13 Interns are only paid expenses.

8.5 ◄))
1 I worked as **an** intern at Beales.
2 I know **the** café you mean.
3 There's **a** printer on the second floor.
4 Jon hasn't got **a** diploma.
5 The CEO is in **the** NY office this week.
6 He's **an** amazing architect.
7 I just started **a** new job.
8 I'd like to put **an** ad in the paper.
9 Have you read **the** job description?
10 I work at **the** theater next door.
11 **The** new café does great coffee.
12 Where is **the** presentation?
13 The Tate is **an** art gallery.
14 I like **the** new CEO.

8.6
Ⓐ 7
Ⓑ 1
Ⓒ 4
Ⓓ 2
Ⓔ 6
Ⓕ 3
Ⓖ 8
Ⓗ 5

8.7 ◄))
1 I've **got three** years' experience.
2 I don't have **a** degree in business studies.
3 He has **a** diploma in economics.
4 I saw **an** ad in The Echo.
5 She has **an** excellent phone manner.
6 He works in **a** hospital.
7 I don't **like interviews**.
8 **The** agency is in the market place.
9 We are looking **for sales people**.

09

9.1 ◄))
1 sales manager
2 librarian
3 doctor
4 hairdresser / stylist
5 engineer
6 train driver
7 writer
8 cleaner / janitor
9 chef
10 electrician
11 mechanic
12 pilot
13 waitress
14 vet
15 travel agent
16 plumber
17 artist
18 judge
19 sales assistant
20 musician
21 surgeon
22 receptionist
23 tour guide
24 taxi driver
25 designer
26 scientist
27 firefighter

9.2 🔊

1. shift
2. apprentice
3. full-time (F/T)
4. temporary
5. co-worker / colleague
6. part-time (P/T)

10

10.1 🔊

1. I love food, and I enjoy cooking.
2. I love working with computers.
3. I enjoy driving.
4. I enjoy traveling to different countries.
5. I don't like working on my own.

10.2 🔊

1. She loves **meeting** new clients.
2. He **doesn't** enjoy giving presentations.
3. I hate **training** big groups.
4. They like **working** in a team.
5. Jan **enjoys** working with children.
6. Ali doesn't **like** long meetings.
7. We don't **like** working weekends.
8. I love **solving** problems.
9. Jim doesn't **enjoy** business trips.

10.3

1. Dislikes
2. Likes
3. Likes
4. Dislikes
5. Likes
6. Dislikes
7. Likes

10.4 🔊

1. I **don't** enjoy work social trips.
2. They like **meeting** new people.
3. He doesn't **like** working late.
4. She hates **sitting** at a desk all day.
5. Do you enjoy **working** in a team?
6. We enjoy **giving** presentations.
7. Angus doesn't like **using** computers.

11

11.1 🔊

1. There are three printers in your department.
2. Are there ladies' toilets on the second floor?
3. There isn't a cafeteria in the building.
4. Is there a set time for lunch breaks?
5. There aren't any elevators in the office.
6. Is there a dress code at this company?
7. There's a photocopier on the first floor.
8. There aren't any trash cans in the office.
9. Are there any interns on your team?
10. There is a calendar on the notice board.

11.2 🔊

1. There is an elevator that goes to all the office floors.
2. There are some stickers in the stationery cabinet.
3. There are some men's toilets on the first and third floors.
4. There is a water cooler in the kitchen.
5. There isn't a set time for lunch breaks.

11.3

1. False
2. True
3. False
4. True
5. False
6. Not given

11.4 🔊

1. There **are** two positions available at our company.
2. There isn't **a** toaster in the kitchen, but there is a microwave.
3. **Is** there a spare computer I can use?
4. Are there **any** pencils in the stationery cabinet?
5. There **is** a big meeting room in our new office.

12

12.1 🔊

1. safe
2. transfer money
3. receipt
4. cash machine / ATM
5. bank
6. currency
7. wallet
8. mobile banking
9. bills (US) / notes (UK)
10. check (US) / cheque (UK)
11. cash register (US) / till (UK)
12. withdraw money
13. invoice
14. online banking
15. credit card

12.2 🔊

1. overtime
2. salary
3. benefits
4. a raise (US) / a pay rise (UK)
5. to earn
6. a bonus
7. annual vacation (US) / annual leave (UK)
8. hourly rate
9. a pay cut

13

13.1 🔊

1. The new intern seems really bright and she is **very organized.**
2. My manager doesn't ask **nervous employees** to give presentations.
3. My director **is very bossy** and she is also hardworking.
4. Sue and Robin are sometimes **rude** to our clients.
5. It's important to stay **calm under pressure**, even if you're very busy.

6 Mushira is very **intelligent**, and she will bring a great deal to the team.

7 It's impossible to feel relaxed when you work with **impatient people**.

8 The people on my team are all very **motivated**, and it's great to work with them.

9 We are looking for a **creative designer** to join our busy production team.

13.2 ◀))

1 Ian seems very hardworking.

2 Kay and Jack are really polite.

3 Ben is very bossy.

4 Diane always looks well dressed.

5 Alex is really impatient.

6 Lenny is a creative chef.

7 This is a great team.

8 Jo seems very organized.

9 Harry seems very bright.

13.3

1 creative

2 organized

3 calm

4 well dressed

13.4 ◀))

1 **Our** team meetings are always interesting.

2 Is this **your** desk? It's very messy!

3 **My** team is very motivated.

4 Is that **their** design? It's great.

5 Kevin is talking to **his** manager.

6 That's Tanya. **Her** phone manner is excellent.

7 The company is very proud of **its** reputation.

13.5 ◀))

1 Is this **his** desk?

2 We don't like **their** product.

3 **My** manager is very smart.

4 This report is **yours**.

5 Jane does **her** job well.

6 They are proud of **their** reputation.

7 Is this tablet **hers**?

8 **Their** manager is never late.

9 Is this **your** pen?

13.6 ◀))

1 The interns have just finished college.

2 Jorge's reputation is well deserved.

3 Nuala's assistant is very helpful.

4 Helen's manager often works late.

5 Maria's co-workers are really friendly.

6 The team members are hardworking.

7 Look at this ad. I like its design.

8 Leroy's work is very impressive.

9 Are there any files in the cabinet?

10 John's confidence has grown this year.

11 Sam's presentation went really well.

12 The CEO's new assistant is very bright.

13 Their products are very popular.

14 That's my boss's parking space.

15 Pablo's report is almost finished.

16 The company is pleased with its new logo.

17 Ethan's team is working on a new project.

13.7 ◀))

1. You are my boss.
2. You are my co-worker.
3. You are Peter's boss.
4. You are Peter's co-worker.
5. You are very polite.
6. You are really polite.
7. They are very polite.
8. They are really polite.
9. Alex is my boss.
10. Alex is my co-worker.
11. Alex is Peter's boss.
12. Alex is Peter's co-worker.
13. Alex is very polite.
14. Alex is really polite.

14

14.1 ◀))

1 Vihaan is very **satisfied** with his office.

2 The new login system is rather **annoying**.

3 The quarterly results are **shocking**.

4 The economic situation is quite **worrying**.

5 We're **excited** about the new office.

6 Simone was **tired** after the course.

7 The profits were **disappointing**.

8 John is **confused** about the schedule.

9 We were **surprised** by the results.

10 We thought the meeting was **boring**.

11 I'm often **exhausted** by Friday.

14.2 ◀))

1 boring

2 confused

3 exciting

4 annoying

5 surprising

6 interesting

7 disappointed

8 worried

14.3 ◀))

1 I am very **busy** with the new project, but I'll be even **busier** next week.

2 Our new office is **large**, but the office in Beijing is **larger**.

3 My job is very **stressful**, but being unemployed is **more stressful**.

4 The meeting was **long**, but last week's was even **longer**.

5 John's flight ticket was **expensive**, but mine was **more expensive**.

6 Our new photocopier is **fast**, but the HR department's is **faster**.

7 Claire's news was **surprising**, but Peter resigning was **more surprising**.

8 My current job is **interesting**, but my old one was **more interesting**.

9 The new furniture is **comfortable**, but the furniture at G-Tech is **more comfortable**.

10 This test is **difficult**, but the next one will be **more difficult**.

11 My commute is **short**; it's only 10 minutes. Pete's is even **shorter**.

14.4 ◀))

1 Your printer is **quicker** than ours.

2 Today's meeting was **more interesting** than usual.

3 Growth was **worse** than we had expected.

4 Sandra has been **more successful** than last year.

5 I'm feeling **better** after a week off work.

6 There is **less** juice left than I thought.

7 My new apartment is **closer** to the center.

8 The results are **better** than in the first quarter.

9 We have an **earlier** start than usual today.

10 Liam has taken a much **later** lunch break than everyone else.

11 This restaurant is **worse** than the others.

12 The flight was **more expensive** than I expected.

14.5 ◀))

1 The new intern is **more helpful than the old one**.

2 Our hours are longer **than those in the German branch**.

3 The new computers are **faster than the old ones**.

4 I feel better **now that I have a new job**.

5 Our new office design **is more modern than the previous one**.

6 The tickets **are more expensive than they used to be**.

7 My raise was **smaller than last year's**.

8 My training this year was **more interesting than last year**.

9 The office is busier **since we merged with our competitors**.

14.6

1 False
2 True
3 False
4 Not given
5 True
6 True
7 False
8 Not given

15

15.1 ◀))

1 Karen leaves home at 7am on Fridays.
2 Vicky usually takes notes during meetings.
3 We don't work the week before New Year.
4 The team always arrives before 10am.
5 Chang arrives at 8:30am every morning.
6 We sometimes have meetings in the evening.
7 Terry sometimes works on the weekend.

15.2 ◀))

1 Everyone arrives **by** 9:30am.
2 Peter often works **until** 11pm.
3 The office is closed **during** August.
4 The café is open **from** 6am.
5 I finish work at 4pm **on** Fridays.
6 The cafeteria is open **from** 1pm.
7 Ann sends an agenda **before** each meeting.

15.3

1 7am
2 1 hour
3 8:30am
4 2pm
5 sometimes
6 afternoon

15.4 ◀))

1 I drive because it's so **convenient**.
2 Jim **takes** the bus every morning.
3 Jack travels **by** bike when he can.
4 The **rush** hour starts at 7am in my city.
5 Sam **takes** the metro home each evening.
6 Raymond **drives** his car to work.
7 I get **on** the bus near the museum.
8 I missed my **connection**.
9 Janet prefers to travel **by** train to work.
10 Karl **takes** the bus home at night.

11 There are a lot of traffic **jams** in the city.
12 You should get **off** the tram at the library.
13 It's much cheaper to **cycle** than drive.
14 I like to **walk** to work in the summer.
15 I prefer to **cycle** to my office.

15.5 ◀))

1 I drive to work.
2 We take the bus.
3 Doug rides his bike to work.
4 I sometimes take a taxi home.
5 The buses run from 5am to 11pm.
6 I go by train.
7 The train arrives at 5pm.
8 Sharon gets off the bus by the station.
9 I like to go home from work on foot.
10 My train to work arrives at 7:45am.
11 Traveling by train is comfortable.
12 The train leaves at about 8pm.
13 I travel by train every day.

15.6

A 1
B 7
C 2
D 4
E 3
F 6
G 5
H 8

15.7 ◀))

1 There aren't many buses **on the weekend**.
2 Hank takes the bus because **it's cheaper than the train**.
3 The office stays open **until 10 in the evening**.
4 I leave for work **between 7 and 8am**.
5 Sally often walks to work **during the summer**.
6 I take the train to work because **it's faster than the bus**.
7 Ted takes notes **during meetings**.
8 I always go to bed **before 11pm**.

16.1 ◄))
1 Saturday
2 Monday
3 Sunday
4 Friday
5 Tuesday
6 Thursday

16.2 ◄))
1 three times a week
2 hourly
3 monthly
4 daily
5 in the morning
6 in the afternoon
7 in the evening
8 before work
9 after work

16.3 ◄))
1 see a play
2 do yoga
3 draw
4 meet friends
5 walk / hike
6 go out for a meal
7 play an instrument
8 watch a movie
9 stay (at) home
10 visit a museum / an art gallery
11 read
12 cook
13 play sports
14 take photos
15 go shopping
16 go camping
17 write
18 go cycling
19 play board games

17.1 ◄))
1 We often go camping on the weekend.
2 Doug sometimes meets friends after he finishes work.
3 I always go running in the morning.
4 My father never watches television.
5 She occasionally sees a play at our local theater.
6 Frank is very lazy, and he rarely does any exercise.
7 My kids sometimes play video games after school.

17.2
1 rarely   2 usually   3 often   4 never

17.3 ◄))
1 Mariam usually stays **at home on weekends**.
2 I sometimes take **photos when I go on vacation**.
3 Dan rarely reads **a newspaper in the morning**.
4 She occasionally sees **a play at her local theater**.
5 Marco usually does **some exercises when he gets up**.
6 I sometimes listen to **music while I travel to work**.
7 We sometimes go out **for a meal at the Chinese restaurant**.
8 I often watch **a movie when I get home from work**.

17.4 ◄))
1 The earliest flight is at 9am.
2 Sydney is the largest city in Australia.
3 Dubai is the hottest place I've visited.
4 This is the most expensive software we sell.
5 The farthest I've flown is to New Zealand.
6 Spanish is the easiest language to learn.
7 Kraków is the most beautiful city in Poland.

8 The train is the most affordable way to travel.
9 This is the most interesting gallery in town.
10 Hiroshi is the most intelligent person I know.
11 That was the scariest film I've seen.

17.5 ◄))
1 The **longest** river in Brazil is the Amazon.
2 We'll have lunch at the **closest** café to the office.
3 I just watched the **worst** presentation I've ever seen.
4 I think that snowboarding is the **most exciting** sport.
5 Sean lives the **farthest** / **furthest** from the office.
6 Antonio is our **most loyal** employee.
7 This is the **most expensive** printer we have.

17.6
1 Dan
2 Pete
3 Pete
4 Pete
5 Dan
6 Chloe
7 Pete
8 Dan
9 Chloe
10 Dan

18.1 ◄))
1 I didn't learn Spanish at school.
2 We walked to the conference center.
3 John lived in New York for 10 years.
4 Did the team discuss the merger?
5 He went to the conference by car.
6 My manager didn't visit the factory.
7 Selma didn't walk to work today.
8 Jimish posted the report a week ago.
9 Did Tom finish the report?

18.2 🔊

Note: "did not" can also be written in contracted form.

1 Akiko **finished** her presentation, then she **watched** some TV.

2 I **did not watch** the game because I **needed** to prepare for the conference.

3 Derek **wanted** to work somewhere interesting, so he **moved** to New York.

4 We **arrived** late, but we **did not miss** the meeting.

5 Sally **passed** her exams, and **decided** to go to college.

18.3 🔊

1 Fred showed me the new conference center.

2 We watched an interesting documentary about Beijing.

3 Ramon started at this company about five years ago.

4 Did you enjoy the presentation about the Indian economy?

5 It rained yesterday, so we didn't play soccer.

6 Arnold cooked me a delicious dinner last night.

7 Did Sam finish the report about the new product range?

8 I booked a table in a restaurant in the center.

9 Did Mike play tennis with the new CEO on Saturday?

18.4 🔊

1 Did Paul start working for us more than five years ago?

2 Did Sally explain how to use the new photocopier?

3 Did it rain while they were in Indonesia?

4 Did Clive pick up the guests from the railway station?

5 Did Mark join you for lunch at the Chinese restaurant?

6 Did the team attend the conference in Paris last year?

7 Did Philip play golf with the consultants last weekend?

8 Did Carl and Marie walk to work again today?

9 Did you watch the game yesterday?

10 Did Janet show you the new photocopier?

11 Did Mo study economics at Stanford University?

12 Did the company invest $10 million in R&D?

18.5

1 False

2 True

3 Not given

4 Not given

5 False

6 True

7 False

18.6 🔊

1 He studied for an exam.

2 She visited a friend.

3 She walked to work.

4 He traveled to India.

5 He listened to the radio.

19

19.1 🔊

1 A

2 A

3 B

4 A

5 B

19.2 🔊

1 It's nine seventeen. / It's seventeen minutes past nine.

2 It's seven o'clock. / It's seven.

3 It's half past five. / It's five thirty.

4 It's three twenty-two. / It's twenty-two minutes past three.

5 It's a quarter to six. / It's five forty-five.

19.3 🔊

1 The soccer tournament ends on June 20.

2 American Independence Day is on the 4th of July.

3 Christmas Day is on December 25.

4 My wife's birthday is on September 5.

5 My daughter was born on August 3.

19.4

1 2014

2 August 2015

3 July

4 Scotland

5 May 3

20

20.1 🔊

1 spent

2 met

3 got

4 went

5 was / were

6 left

7 told

8 thought

9 said

10 began

11 chose

20.2 🔊

1 I **went** to Paris on a business trip last week.

2 I **spent** all afternoon working on a report.

3 I **began** working at Carter's last year.

4 The CEO **told** me that my work was excellent.

5 I **thought** this project was very difficult.

6 Besim **was** off sick yesterday.

7 I **met** the new Sales Director this morning.

8 The staff **chose** the name of the company.

9 Kara **left** her last job because it was boring.

20.3 🔊
1 I **met** the International Marketing Director last week.
2 I **had** a demanding boss.
3 I **left** my last job because it was badly paid.
4 I **got** to work very early today.
5 They **went** to the New York office last month.
6 The staff **chose** new chairs for the office.
7 Sally **thought** that Rohit's presentation went well.

20.4 🔊
1 I started work there after I left school.
2 I worked in a bank at the start of my career.
3 I took the children to school.
4 I met many interesting people.
5 I worked hard and studied for an MBA.
6 We had a black and white uniform.

20.5
A 7
B 1
C 2
D 8
E 3
F 5
G 4
H 6

20.6 🔊
1 I **felt** very well respected by my team leader.
2 The Head of Sales **taught** me to give interesting presentations.
3 My brother **made** a delicious cake, which I took to work for my birthday.
4 The staff **chose** the pictures for the meeting rooms, and they look great.
5 I **left** my last job because I didn't get along with the customers.
6 I **spent** all of yesterday writing a sales report and now I'm very tired.

21

21.1 🔊
1 We **launched** a new range of apps last year.
2 At **first**, we only had four employees.
3 Two years **ago**, we opened our tenth store.
4 The company **merged** with a competitor a year ago.
5 A new Director of Marketing **started** working here last year.

21.2 🔊
1 **At first**, we only had one store.
2 We **opened** a new flagship store last month.
3 We **launched** an exciting new app last year.
4 A new Director of HR started working six months **ago**.

21.3
1 Over 10,000
2 In her garage
3 50
4 Two years ago
5 At craft fairs

21.4
1 last month
2 during the first quarter
3 in the winter of 2012
4 recently

21.5 🔊
1 **Last** spring, sales of umbrellas **rose** because it was wet.
2 UK sales **went up** in 2011, but **fell** in 2012.
3 **At** first, the value of shares in the company **remained** steady.
4 Online marketing costs **increased** and sales also **rose**.

22

22.1 🔊
1 to accept an invitation
2 to attend a meeting
3 calendar
4 boardroom
5 to invite someone
6 office
7 conference room
8 running late
9 restaurant
10 reception
11 café
12 morning
13 afternoon
14 evening
15 appointment
16 refreshments
17 to decline an invitation
18 to miss a meeting
19 agenda

22.2 🔊
1 to come up
2 to cancel
3 to be busy
4 to be unable to attend
5 to look forward to
6 to reschedule

23

23.1 🔊
1 The company **is losing** money, so we **are planning** a restructure.
2 Stacy **is not working** in the office today. She **is visiting** the factory.
3 Dan **is meeting** a new client. They **are chatting** in the meeting room.
4 Colin **is starting** a new project. He **is working** with Angela.
5 The head office **is relocating** to Delhi. We **are moving** this week.

⑥ Profits **are falling** this year, and the team **is feeling** nervous.

⑦ Anika **is working** late tonight. She **is preparing** a presentation.

⑧ Sue and Clive **are having** lunch downtown. They **are eating** Chinese.

⑨ I **am going** on vacation next week. I **am missing** the training day.

⑩ Our company **is selling** a lot to India. We **are opening** an office in Mumbai.

⑪ Our secretary **is retiring**. We **are recruiting** a new one.

⑫ Sam and Sue **are discussing** the report. They **are planning** a meeting about it.

⑬ Chrissie **is choosing** a new team. She **is considering** Paul for a position.

⑭ Alex **is leaving** the company. He **is moving** to New York.

23.2 ◄))
① Who are you meeting?
② Is Tim writing the report?
③ Are Kim and Jo presenting today?
④ Are you printing the agenda?
⑤ Is the company moving?
⑥ When are you retiring?
⑦ Who are you promoting?

23.3 ◄))
① Is the conference taking place in Venice next April?
② Is Leanne giving a presentation on the takeover plans?
③ Are our owners hoping to buy our biggest competitor?
④ Is Brendan programming the software for new machinery?
⑤ Are we taking time off in August this year?

23.4 ◄))
① Are you having lunch at 1pm today?
② Tom is going to the conference today.
③ Is John working until 7pm again?
④ We are traveling to New York again.
⑤ Are you coming to the meeting on Friday?

⑥ Are you visiting the factory next month?
⑦ I'm not taking time off in August.
⑧ The head office is moving in the spring.
⑨ Fran isn't coming to the office tomorrow.
⑩ What are you doing on Tuesday?
⑪ Sam is meeting the client this afternoon.
⑫ Tim is leaving work at 5pm today.

23.5
① On Monday morning, Frank is **visiting the factory**.
② On Monday afternoon, Clare is **attending a course**.
③ On Tuesday, Frank is **celebrating his wedding anniversary**.
④ In the evening, he is **going to the theater**.
⑤ On Thursday at 2pm, Clare is **meeting Pete**.
⑥ They are both free at **2:30pm on Thursday**.

23.6 ◄))
① I'm having lunch with the IT team.
② I'm meeting them at 3pm.
③ I'm flying to Edinburgh.
④ I'm returning to London at 11:30am.
⑤ I'm going to Sandra's leaving party.

24

24.1 ◄))
① Polite
② Impolite
③ Polite
④ Polite
⑤ Polite
⑥ Impolite
⑦ Polite

24.2
① True
② False
③ True
④ False
⑤ Not given
⑥ False
⑦ Not given

24.3 ◄))
① I'm sorry. I'm not sure I **agree**.
② Sorry, but in my **opinion** they will sell well.
③ I can see your **point**, but I still think senior citizens are more important.
④ If I could just **come** in here and mention the good news from France.
⑤ **Excuse** me, but my figures tell a different story.
⑥ **Could** I just say...? The budget won't cover it.
⑦ I'm not **sure** I agree. Sales to China are growing faster.
⑧ Sorry to **interrupt**, but the software is not ready yet.

24.4 ◄))
① I'm afraid Sean can't make it to the meeting and has **sent** his apologies.
② Shall we **take** a vote on the new strategy to see what course of action to take?
③ Ramona will **take** the minutes and email them to everyone after the meeting.
④ I agree with the motion. How **about** you? What do you think about it?
⑤ If I could just **interrupt** for a moment. I think we need to take a vote on this.
⑥ That sums up most of the issues we are facing. I just have a few **closing** remarks.
⑦ Claude is the chair, so he has the **casting** vote if there is a tie.
⑧ The **chair** of our budget meetings likes to keep his closing remarks very short.
⑨ I read **through** the agenda before the meeting, so I know what we will be talking about.

24.5 🔊

1. footprint
2. green
3. reuse
4. resources
5. waste
6. environment
7. reduce

25

25.1 🔊

1. Me neither.
2. Neither do I.
3. So did I.
4. Neither did I.
5. Me too.
6. So do I.
7. Me neither.
8. So do I.
9. Me too.

25.2 🔊

1. I suppose so. It will be expensive though.
2. So did I. He's so entertaining.
3. I agree. The team could improve their skills.
4. I'll ask the secretary to send it again.
5. Me neither. The food's very bland.
6. So do I. It's very comfortable.
7. Exactly. I didn't understand it at all.
8. I agree. I learned some new skills.
9. Absolutely. We should promote her.

25.3 🔊

1. I'm **afraid** we'll have to cancel the meeting.
2. I'm sorry, but I **disagree** with you.
3. I **totally** disagree with you about this.
4. I'm really not **sure** about that design.
5. I'm **sorry**, Pete, but I don't agree with you.
6. I don't agree at **all**. It won't work.
7. I'm not **sure** about this. Can we talk later?

8. I'm afraid I **don't** agree with you at all.
9. I don't **agree** at all with the merger.
10. You **could** be right, but I'm not sure.
11. Sorry, but I disagree **with** this plan.

25.4

1. Greg disagrees with her.
2. Greg thinks he doesn't have enough experience.
3. Jenny strongly disagrees.
4. Greg agrees.
5. Jenny strongly agrees.

25.5 🔊

1. We **totally** agree about the redesign.
2. I can't agree with you **at** all about the downsizing.
3. We're **afraid** we totally disagree.
4. You **could** be right, but I need more evidence.
5. I'm not sure **about** the latest business plan.

26

26.1 🔊

1. Roger hurt himself when he slipped.
2. She burned herself on the coffee maker.
3. Ron blames himself for the accident.
4. Jan cut herself on the machinery.
5. We enjoyed ourselves at the office party.
6. Juan cut himself in the kitchen.
7. We need to protect ourselves from risks.

26.2 🔊

1. I hurt **myself** when I moved the photocopier.
2. They should prepare **themselves** for the course.
3. Claire's cut **herself** on the equipment.
4. Have you all signed **yourselves** up for the course?
5. Sam is teaching **himself** Japanese.

26.3

1. Not given
2. Not given
3. True
4. False
5. Not given
6. False
7. True
8. False

26.4 🔊

1. An **extinguisher** is used to stop small fires.
2. If you hear the fire alarm, go to the **assembly area**.
3. Medical equipment is kept in the **first aid kit**.
4. Each fire **escape** has a sign above the door.
5. You practice leaving the building during a **fire drill**.

27

27.1 🔊

1. How about asking Tim to write the report?
2. Why don't we ask Pete for his opinion?
3. We could have a meeting on Friday.
4. Let's ask the team for their opinions.
5. What about putting some videos online?
6. Why don't we hire another intern?
7. How about moving the meeting to 5pm?
8. Let's try calling the engineer again.

27.2 🔊

1. She should go home and rest.
2. You should ask the secretary for another.
3. You should go on a training course.
4. You should order some more.
5. He should call IT.
6. You should call the engineer.
7. You should ask for an extension.
8. You should take the bus.

27.3 🔊

❶ Where have the reports gone? They've **disappeared**.

❷ Pete **misunderstood** me. He thought I said 3 o'clock.

❸ Cathy isn't coming in today. She's feeling **unwell**.

❹ You should be **careful** crossing the road.

❺ Doug is really **impatient**. He gets angry so easily.

❻ I'm **unable** to come to the training because I have a meeting.

❼ Don't forget to **disconnect** the machine after you've used it.

❽ I'm **unfamiliar** with that program. I don't know it.

❾ Jean is so **careless**. She's always making mistakes.

❿ This morning is **impractical** for me. Can we meet later?

27.4 🔊

❶ We should make sure no one **misunderstood** the instructions.

❷ How about organizing training for everyone who is **unfamiliar** with the program?

❸ Let's make sure no one on the team **spells** the name wrongly again.

❹ Why don't we ask Pete to help if Laura isn't **well** tomorrow?

❺ I think we should **disconnect** the machine since it's not working.

❻ I don't think you should be so **impatient** with the new recruits.

❼ Let's send a memo to everyone who isn't **able** to come to the meeting.

❽ Let's explain to Tim that he should be more **careful** with financial information.

❾ Why don't we try to find a time that is **convenient** for everyone?

28

28.1

❶ young adults
❷ sports wear
❸ jackets
❹ 65%
❺ 80%
❻ China
❼ India

28.2 🔊

❶ Today I'm going to talk about profit.
❷ Does anyone have any questions?
❸ To sum up, we are facing issues.
❹ I'm happy to answer questions.
❺ Last, let's look at the future.

28.3 🔊

❶ I'd like to begin **by showing you this graph**.

❷ I'm happy to **answer any questions**.

❸ Does anyone have any more **questions or comments**?

❹ Let's move **on to the next topic**.

❺ After that, I would **like to talk about the merger**.

❻ To sum up, it's **been an excellent quarter for the company**.

28.4 🔊

❶ The **screen** is black. We can't see the graph.

❷ If you use a **projector**, you can introduce graphs and visuals.

❸ I'll write down the company's name on the **flipchart**.

❹ There are programs to help you make professional-looking **slides**.

❺ If you use a **microphone**, the people at the back will hear you.

28.5 🔊

❶ I'd **like** to start with our factory in Vietnam.

❷ To sum **up**, we need to invest more in infrastructure.

❸ I'll **explore** the benefits of investing in web technology later.

❹ Let's begin **by** looking at the sales figures.

❺ In **short**, we need to develop new products.

❻ Let's take a **look** at the second graph.

❼ So we've **covered** all the topics I wanted to discuss.

❽ Turning **to** the previous quarter's profits.

❾ Then I'm going to **talk** about the situation in China.

❿ **To** start, let's look at this year's performance.

⓫ Moving **on**, let's look at our main competitors.

⓬ First, I'm going to look **at** last year's results.

⓭ I'm happy to **answer** any questions at the end.

⓮ I'd like to end **by** thanking you all for your attention today.

29

29.1 🔊

❶ You **don't have to** stay late tonight. It's very quiet.

❷ Is your phone broken? You **can** use mine if you like.

❸ We **have to** wear a jacket and tie when we meet clients.

❹ You **can't** park there. It's a space for disabled drivers.

29.2 🔊

❶ You can't leave early tonight. **We have an important meeting at 5pm.**

❷ You don't have to pay for lunch. **Staff eat for free in the cafeteria.**

❸ You can make yourself a hot drink. **There's tea and coffee in the kitchen.**

❹ We have to wear business clothes. **There's a formal dress code.**

5 We have to leave the building now. **That's the fire alarm.**

29.3
1 True
2 False
3 Not given
4 True
5 False

29.4 ◀))
1 I **can listen** to music at work if I use headphones.
2 He's a pilot. He **has** to wear a uniform.
3 They **don't have** to go to the training session.
4 He can't **take** more than an hour for his lunch break.
5 He **can't** leave early. It's too busy.
6 I have **to** back up my files before I turn my computer off.

29.5 ◀))
1 Could you wash these cups, please?
2 Would you mind turning the light off?
3 Could you help me lift this box, please?
4 Would you mind calling me back later?
5 Could you lend me your stapler, please?

29.6 ◀))
1 Could you open the window?
2 Would you mind checking this list?
3 Could you forward me Jo's email?
4 Would you mind printing the report?
5 Could you pass around the agenda?
6 Would you mind ordering more files?
7 Could you come to today's meeting?

29.7 ◀))
1 Could you turn your music down?
2 Would you mind checking my report for me?
3 Could you close the window?
4 Would you mind inviting Alan to the meeting?

29.8 ◀))
1 Could you check these sales figures?
2 Would you mind paying a deposit now?
3 Could you ask Ian to call me back?
4 Would you mind showing our clients around?

29.9 ◀))
1 Would you mind **opening** the door? It's really hot in here.
2 Would you mind **asking** John to email me this month's sales figures?
3 Could you **take** the minutes for this afternoon's meeting?
4 Could you **remind** me who is coming to tomorrow's presentation?

30

30.1 ◀))
1 to think outside the box
2 to get down to business
3 red tape
4 to take it easy
5 to be tied up with
6 to wind down
7 business as usual
8 to be out of order
9 a win-win situation
10 to be in the red
11 to work around the clock
12 the ball is in your court
13 to put something off
14 going haywire
15 throwing money down the drain
16 to be swamped
17 to pull your weight

31

31.1 ◀))
1 Tanya was feeling very tired.
2 I was finishing his report.
3 Alison was talking to the CEO.
4 Was Jamie taking minutes?
5 Were you working late yesterday?
6 I was trying to call you.
7 Claire was playing very loud music.

31.2 ◀))
Note: Negative answers can also use long forms.
1 The train trip here was really bad. All the trains **were running** late.
2 The cleaners **were complaining** that staff left their dirty cups in the sink.
3 Harriet **wasn't listening** to the presentation.
4 Tom's manager was annoyed because Tom **wasn't meeting** his deadlines.
5 My email inbox **was getting** full, so I had to delete some messages.

31.3
1 True
2 False
3 True
4 True
5 False

31.4 ◀))
1 Joshua **was giving** a talk about new markets.
2 Fiona **wasn't listening** to Bilal's new ideas for products.
3 Lucia **was taking** the minutes of the meeting.
4 They **were speaking** too loudly on the phone.
5 Helen **was eating** her lunch at her desk.

31.5
1 The windows
2 Talking

③ Her assistant
④ Her USB cable
⑤ Talk to a co-worker
⑥ Think clearly

32

32.1 ◀))
① I am so sorry I was late for the meeting with our clients today.
② I would like to apologize for not finishing the report yesterday.
③ I'm really sorry. I forgot to charge the office cell phone and it has no power.
④ I'm really sorry this line is so bad. I hope we don't get cut off.
⑤ I'm afraid that's not good enough. I want a full refund on my ticket.

32.2 ◀))
① No problem. I'll help you finish it now.
② That's not good enough. Please heat it up.
③ Never mind. We're not very busy today.
④ No problem. I'll have tea instead.
⑤ Don't worry. I'll print off some more.

32.3
Ⓐ 4
Ⓑ 3
Ⓒ 1
Ⓓ 5
Ⓔ 2

32.4 ◀))
① I'm really **sorry**. I forgot to send the agenda for the meeting.
② I would like to **apologize** for the rudeness of the waitress.
③ I'm **afraid** that's not good enough. You missed an important meeting.
④ That's all **right**. I'll make you a copy right now.
⑤ Please **make** sure it doesn't happen again.

⑥ Never **mind**. It's only a cup.
⑦ I would **like** to apologize for the delay to your train this evening.

32.5 ◀))
① Harry **was practicing** his presentation when I **called** him.
② Sam's cell phone **rang** when Tom **was describing** the sales for this quarter.
③ The elevator **got** stuck while they **were waiting** for it.
④ Tina **wasn't listening** when the CEO **said** all staff would get a raise.
⑤ The fire alarm **went** off when we **were having** our update meeting.
⑥ I **was working** late when I **heard** a strange noise.
⑦ I **was editing** the report when the fire alarm **went** off.

32.6 ◀))
① The photocopier **broke** while I **was copying** your sales report.
② We **were listening** to Janet's presentation when the power **went** off.
③ John **was signing** the contract when the lawyer **called** him.
④ Anna **was** furious when she found out George **was copying** her ideas.
⑤ Simon **was editing** the report when his computer **crashed**.
⑥ We **were waiting** for the bus when two buses **arrived**.

33

33.1 ◀))
Note: All answers can also be written in contracted form.
① I **have called** eight customers this morning.
② Gareth **has made** coffee for the visitors.
③ Piotr **has cut** the hair of many famous people.

④ I **have not finished** checking my emails.
⑤ Carl **has not emailed** me the sales data.

33.2 ◀))
① She hasn't sent the invoice **yet**.
② We have **just** heard the CEO is leaving.
③ I haven't met the new director **yet**.
④ Has Tom finished fixing my laptop **yet**?
⑤ George has **just** called me.
⑥ The painters haven't finished **yet**.
⑦ Have you had a meeting with Ann **yet**?
⑧ The trainer has **just** arrived.
⑨ Have you **just** finished the report?

33.3 ◀))
① I haven't ordered the stationery yet.
② They have just introduced the new packaging.
③ Have you answered those emails yet?
④ Derinda has just written the minutes from our meeting.

33.4
① True
② False
③ True
④ Not given

33.5 ◀))
① Daniel **sent** your package last Friday.
② Jenny **showed** me the new designs yesterday.
③ Babu and Zack **haven't finished** their research yet.
④ Kate **spoke** to the HR manager last week.

33.6
① B
② A
③ B
④ A
⑤ A

33.7 🔊
1. I have done all the invoices for June.
2. He met the Chinese partners last month.
3. He hasn't sent the salaries to payroll yet.
4. They have not started the audit yet.
5. He left this morning.
6. I have just heard about your promotion.
7. She has sold the most products.
8. Have you designed that box yet?
9. They have given him a verbal warning.
10. Mark hasn't scanned it yet.
11. I have spoken to your team.

33.8 🔊
1. Yes, I've **just** scanned them.
2. No, he **hasn't** done them yet.
3. **I've** filed them all in the cabinet.
4. We've **stopped** the delivery.

34

34.1 🔊
1. We will replace your tablet free of charge.
2. The chef will cook you another pizza.
3. I'll talk to the boss about it.
4. The manager will be with you soon.
5. I'll contact our courier immediately.
6. We will give you a full refund.
7. I promise that your order will arrive today.
8. I'm afraid we won't finish the project on time.
9. I'm sorry, but we won't cancel your order.

34.2 🔊
1. We'll send it to your hotel when it gets here.
2. I'll ask the chef to cook it properly.
3. I'll refund the money to your credit card.
4. I will call the driver immediately.
5. We'll move you to another room.

34.3
1. There was no receptionist
2. They will ask receptionists to work late
3. The bathroom was dirty
4. He will speak to the cleaners' manager
5. There wasn't any hot coffee
6. Mr. Vance was kept awake
7. A full refund

34.4 🔊
1. We'll offer you a discount off your next hotel stay.
2. Will the money be refunded to my credit card?
3. The company will chase your order up for you.
4. The store manager will be with you very soon.
5. Will you replace the part on my broken washing machine?

34.5
1. Won't
2. Will
3. Will
4. Won't

34.6 🔊
1. I'm very sorry about that. **We'll offer** you a refund.
2. I really must apologize. I**'ll take** it back to the kitchen.
3. She**'ll be** with you in a minute.
4. I**'ll talk** to her about this.
5. It **won't happen** again.
6. I**'ll ask** the chef to make you something vegetarian.

35

35.1 🔊
1. bus
2. plane
3. helicopter
4. tram
5. bus stop
6. car
7. taxi
8. airport
9. train station
10. taxi stand (US) / taxi rank (UK)
11. bicycle

35.2 🔊
1. terminal
2. security
3. boarding pass
4. on time
5. domestic flight
6. international flight
7. connecting flight
8. delay
9. passport control
10. late
11. hotel
12. board a plane
13. check-in
14. passport
15. luggage
16. round-trip ticket (US) / return ticket (UK)
17. window seat
18. aisle seat
19. seat reservation

36

36.1 🔊
Note: All answers can be written in contracted form.
1. If we **don't hurry**, we **will miss** the flight.
2. If we **meet** in Berlin, it **will save** us some time.
3. We **will take** on a new intern if we **win** the contract.
4. If the train **is** late, we **will miss** the meeting.
5. If the bank **is** closed, we **will not have** any money.
6. We **will pay** for your flight if you **fly** to Denver.

7 If you **work** hard, you **will pass** the exam.

8 The firm **will pay** expenses if you **are** delayed.

9 If I **go** to Rome, I **will visit** the Colosseum.

10 If I **lose** my job, I don't know what I **will do**.

36.2 🔊

1 If we don't hurry up, **we'll miss our connecting flight**.

2 We will get a discount **if we book early**.

3 Will you pay expenses **if we attend the conference**?

4 What will Samantha do if **she loses her job next month**?

5 If we lose the contract, **we will have to lay Sean off**.

6 Will you visit the factory **if you go to China**?

36.3 🔊

1 Will you have a celebration if you get the job?

2 If you buy the ticket online, it will be cheaper.

3 If we visit Paris, we will probably go sightseeing.

4 What will we do if we don't win the contract?

5 If we take on a new intern, where will they sit?

6 How will you travel to Berlin if the flight is canceled?

36.4

1 True
2 False
3 True
4 False
5 Not given
6 True

36.5 🔊

1 If it's a nice day, I walk to work.

2 If you heat water, it boils.

3 If you're late for work, isn't your boss unhappy?

4 If you press that button, the machine stops.

36.6 🔊

1 Will you visit Red Square if you **go** to Moscow?

2 People use public transportation if it **is** cheap.

3 What will we do if we **lose** the contract?

4 The ticket **will be** more expensive if we buy it later.

5 If you **pay** staff more, they work harder.

6 **Will** you pick me up from the station if I give you my details?

7 We'll miss the train if we **don't** hurry.

8 If it **rains**, the event is always moved indoors.

9 Sharon **won't** go on vacation if she loses her job.

10 **Will** Doug resign if the company loses the deal?

37

37.1 🔊

1 Do you know the **way** to the station?

2 The bank is **on** the corner.

3 Do you know how to **get** to the hotel?

4 The museum is **in** front of the park.

5 You should **take** the second left.

6 The library is straight ahead on **the** right.

7 Our house is just ahead **on** the left.

8 Sorry, did you **say** it is near the school?

9 Turn right **at** the sign.

37.2 🔊

1 The entrance is in front of the factory.

2 Turn right at the sign.

3 The bank is opposite the school.

4 Take the first road on the left.

5 Go past the movie theater.

6 The bank is on the corner.

7 The station is next to the police station.

37.3 🔊

1 Excuse me, do you know the way to the hotel?

2 Go straight on and it's opposite the train station.

3 Sorry, did you say it's next to the post office?

4 The bank is 40 yards ahead on the corner.

37.4

1 A
2 B
3 A
4 A
5 B

37.5 🔊 Model Answers

1 Take the first right, and it's on the left after the town hall.

2 Sure, go straight ahead, and it's on the left.

3 Yes, go straight ahead, and it's on the right.

4 Yes, take the first right, and then it's on the right.

5 Turn left, then turn right, and it's on the left.

38

38.1 🔊

1 The hotel was opened in 1932.

2 The new factory was opened by the president.

3 Simon was employed by our company in 2013.

4 Our new range of products will be released next month.

5 Our head office was moved to Shanghai about four years ago.

6 Peter was introduced to the new management team.

7 Coffee and tea will be served during the break.

8 The team will be shown how to use the new software package.

38.2 ◀)) Model Answers
1 The CEO was met at the airport.

2 The meeting room has been redecorated.

3 A double room was booked yesterday.

4 The team was taught some Mandarin.

5 The files were left on the train again.

6 The rooms were booked on Monday.

7 Breakfast is served at 7:30am.

8 The office has been organized.

38.3
A 5
B 1
C 4
D 3
E 2
F 7
G 6
H 8

38.4
1 False
2 Not given
3 True
4 False

38.5 ◀))
1 We **were picked up** at the airport by the driver.

2 Great. It **was served** at 7am each morning.

3 Yes. But unfortunately it **was broken**.

39.1 ◀))
1 fry
2 waiter
3 vegetarian
4 chef
5 waitress
6 menu
7 make a reservation / booking
8 boil
9 receipt
10 breakfast
11 lunch
12 dinner
13 café
14 vegan
15 dessert
16 food allergy / intolerance
17 bar
18 tip
19 roast

39.2 ◀))
1 fruit
2 bread
3 water
4 napkin
5 milk
6 fish
7 coffee
8 pasta
9 tea
10 meat
11 fork
12 knife
13 vegetables
14 seafood
15 salad
16 sandwich
17 potatoes
18 butter
19 cake

40.1 ◀))
1 Did you have any trouble getting here?
2 Can I get you anything?
3 It's great to meet you in person.
4 Have you been to Toronto before?
5 Did you have a good flight?
6 Would you like something to drink?
7 I've been looking forward to meeting you.
8 We've heard so much about you.
9 I'll let Mr. Song know that you arrived.
10 Is this your first visit to India?

40.2 ◀))
1 Is there **any** information about flights?
2 I need to buy **some** food.
3 Are there **any** good hotels nearby?
4 Can I get you **a** cup of coffee?
5 Are there **any** interesting talks today?
6 Do you have **any** luggage?
7 There is **a** presentation later.
8 Do you have **any** tea?
9 Please take **a** seat at the front.

40.3 ◀))
1 Would you like some **water, Mrs. Smith**?
2 Do you have any **information about the flight**?
3 Have you been **to Los Angeles before**?
4 Can I get you **a glass of water**?
5 It's great to **meet you in person**.
6 There isn't **any coffee left, I'm afraid**.

40.4 ◀))
1 Are you going to **any** talks later?
2 James is giving **a** presentation later today.
3 There isn't **any** coffee or tea, I'm sorry.
4 Are **any** of your colleagues staying here?
5 Would you like **a** cup of tea, Jen?
6 They don't have **any** workshops this afternoon.
7 Have **any** of the attendees arrived yet?

8 Is there **any** information about the conference?

9 There's **some** food and drink in the main hall.

40.5

1 the main hall

2 developing an app

3 a choice of food and drink

4 a product launch

5 leading CEOs

6 the Asian market

41

41.1 ◀))

1 I'm afraid we're fully booked this evening.

2 Can we sit outside on the terrace?

3 Could I have a cup of coffee, please?

4 Can we just have five more minutes, please?

5 Yes, I'm allergic to shellfish.

6 Absolutely delicious, thank you.

7 Yes, please. Some chocolate ice cream for me.

8 No, I'm afraid it contains cream.

9 Sure, are you paying by cash or by card?

41.2 ◀))

1 Are you ready to order?

2 I'd like to reserve a table for two, please.

3 Have you reserved a table, madam?

4 How many people are there in your party?

5 Could I have a look at the dessert menu, please?

6 What would you like for the entree?

7 Do you have any allergies or intolerances?

8 How many vegetarian options are there today?

9 Could we have the bill, please?

10 Would you like to pay by cash or card?

41.3 ◀))

1 How many chairs will you need?

2 I ordered too many dishes.

3 There's not enough space here. It's tiny.

4 How many plates will you need?

5 There are too many chairs.

6 There's not enough cake for everyone.

7 The lobster costs too much.

8 We haven't ordered enough dishes.

9 How many guests are you expecting?

10 I don't have enough cash for a tip.

11 I've eaten too much food this evening!

12 There's enough tea for everyone.

41.4 ◀))

1 How **many** people are coming tonight?

2 Is there **enough** space at the table for everyone?

3 How **much** does the meal usually cost?

4 I've eaten too **much** cake.

5 There's **too** much salt in my soup.

6 There are not **enough** chairs for all of us!

7 **How** many glasses will we need this evening?

42

42.1 ◀))

1 I'd **better** go now.

2 Can I **ask** who's calling?

3 No, that's **all**, thanks.

4 OK. **Talk** to you soon.

5 Is there **anything** else I can do?

6 Hello, Sales **department**.

42.2

A 5

B 3

C 2

D 1

E 4

42.3 ◀))

1 Esme speaking. How can I help?

2 Of course. It's Sergio Walker.

3 OK. Speak to you soon.

4 Hi, Andrew. It's José from Design.

42.4

1 57336

2 0114342190

3 031297778

4 0092736430

5 2074440016

6 00340621485

7 8694472165

42.5 ◀))

Model Answers

1 Liz's extension is 3864.

2 Saira's office number is 01928 335178.

3 The Helpdesk number at KTV News is 616 888 3746.

4 Lucy's cell phone number is 616 913 6205.

42.6 ◀))

1 I don't know why Hal's not **picking up** the phone.

2 I'll **put you through** to customer services now.

3 Can you **speak up**, please? I can't hear you.

4 Sorry, I'm busy now. I'll **get back** to you later.

5 I'm sorry I **cut you off**. This line is very bad.

6 You're **breaking up**. Can I call you back?

42.7 ◀))

1 Could you possibly speak **up**, please? The line is very faint.

2 I'll call **you** back in ten minutes. Is that OK? I have to finish writing an email.

3 If I get cut **off**, call me back on the office phone. I'm back at my desk now.

4 Can I get back **to** you about the design later today? We're still working on it.

5 I've called Fatima three times, but she didn't pick **up**. Is she at work today?

6 Marc kept breaking **up** when I called him. The signal here is awful!

7 Katie is back at her desk now. I'll just put you **through** to her.

8 Mateo got back **to** me about the new manual. He has a few comments on it.

42.8 ◀》
1 Can you speak up, please?

2 I hope I don't get cut off again.

3 Let me put you through to Finance.

4 Sorry I didn't pick up when you called.

5 Can you get back to him this afternoon?

6 Sorry, the line keeps breaking up.

7 I'll call you back in five minutes.

8 He didn't get back to me yesterday.

9 Don't pick up the phone if Dan calls.

43

43.1 ◀》
1 Yes, of course. May I ask who's calling?

2 I'm calling because my laptop is broken.

3 Yes. Can you ask her to call me back?

4 Could you ask her to call me back today?

43.2 ◀》
1 **It's** Sunita Devinder from GBT.

2 I wonder if you **could** help me.

3 I'm afraid Mr. Cox **isn't** at his desk.

4 Thank you for **calling** Top Sounds.

5 **Could** I speak to Rod Dean, please?

6 Could you **ask** him to call me back?

7 **May** I ask who's calling, please?

43.3 ◀》
1 How can I help you?

2 May I ask who's calling?

3 I'll just put you through.

4 Would you like to leave a message?

5 Could you ask him to call me back, please?

6 IT department. How can I help you?

---

7 I'll put you through to HR now.

8 I'm afraid he's not at his desk.

9 Thank you for calling Quadfax.

43.4 ◀》
1 Savino's. How **can I help** you?

2 Thank you **for calling** Ready Solutions.

3 Hello. **I wonder if** you can help me.

4 I'm calling **about an order** I placed last month.

5 **Could I speak** to Becky Bradley, please?

6 I'm afraid the Accounts Manager is away **at the moment**.

7 Yes, please. **Could I order** 20 desks?

8 **Would you like** to leave a message?

9 Thank you. **I'll just put** you through.

43.5
OPINION:

nice, **awful**, **stylish**

SIZE:

tiny, **large**, **huge**

AGE:

ancient, **modern**, **antique**

COLOR:

blue, **purple**, **pink**

MATERIAL:

leather, **metal**, **plastic**

43.6 ◀》
1 We're developing a stylish little gold lamp.

2 Tom has got an amazing tiny new smartphone.

3 The pet store has a nice big black and white cat.

4 There is an awful large modern painting in the cafeteria.

5 Have you seen the exciting new colorful marketing posters?

43.7 ◀》
1 That's a stylish new design for the company logo.

2 There's a huge round hole in the wall where the truck hit it.

3 Have you seen the fabulous new office chairs?

---

4 There's a big yellow and red truck outside.

5 There's a nice big green and white plant in my office.

6 Have you tasted the awful new coffee?

7 The headphones for my laptop go in a tiny round hole.

8 There's a large rectangular parking space for motorbikes.

43.8
1 Printed materials

2 Next Tuesday

3 9:00

4 60

5 Six taxis

6 Vegetarian and gluten-free food

44

44.1 ◀》
1 Personal statement

2 Education

3 Professional achievements

4 Career summary

5 Key skills

44.2 ◀》
1 I have a **proven** track record in the tourism industry.

2 I am proficient **in** using a wide range of software.

3 I have hands-on **experience** of customer service.

4 I have experience working in a **service-oriented** environment.

44.3 ◀》
1 I am a highly motivated individual and love working in tourism.

2 I gained in-depth knowledge of the construction industry.

3 I have a great deal of experience in the catering industry.

4 I am proficient in most types of accounting software.

44.4 🔊

1 I **managed** a large team of marketing executives.
2 Our teams **collaborated** to create a new clothing range.
3 The company **established** a new headquarters in the capital.
4 I **negotiated** with our suppliers and got a good deal.

44.5 Model Answers

1 She oversaw the introduction of new accounting software and co-ordinated a training program.
2 She is the Deputy Director of Accounts at Tomkins Travel.
3 She worked in the construction industry.
4 She gained her diploma in Accounting in June 2010.
5 She can speak Spanish and English fluently.

45

45.1 🔊

Note: All answers except **6**, **8**, and **11** can also be written in contracted form.

1 He **is going to travel** to the conference by plane.
2 She **is not going to make** it to the meeting.
3 They **are going to meet** the staff from the Paris office.
4 He **is going to write** a letter to the suppliers.
5 They **are not going to sell** their shares in the company just now.
6 **Is** she **going to order** business cards with the new company logo?
7 Sergio **is going to give** a presentation about the new training course.
8 **Are** you **going to make** tea and coffee for the visitors?
9 Diana **is going to design** the new company logo.
10 They **are going to join** us for our team meeting today.
11 **Are** you **going to review** the sales data this afternoon?

45.2 🔊

1 Why don't we ask what Marketing think?
2 Could you load the printer with paper?
3 Can you help me with these files, please?
4 Could you send the files to production?
5 Could we meet at 4 instead of 5?
6 Can you finish the report today?
7 Couldn't we invite Jeff to the meeting?
8 Could you call me back later, please?
9 Could you make coffee for the CEO?
10 Could we possibly cancel the meeting?
11 Can you check this report, please?
12 Could you pass round the agenda?
13 Can we try a different approach?
14 Please could you call the Delhi office?
15 Could you lock up before you leave?
16 Could you possibly stay late tonight?
17 Please can you print out these designs?

45.3 🔊

1. I am going to email the director.
2. I am going to email the IT help desk.
3. I am going to email the sales department.
4. I am going to speak to the director.
5. I am going to speak to the IT help desk.
6. I am going to speak to the sales department.
7. You are going to email the director.
8. You are going to email the IT help desk.
9. You are going to email the sales department.
10. You are going to speak to the director.
11. You are going to speak to the IT help desk.
12. You are going to speak to the sales department.
13. Kelly is going to email the director.
14. Kelly is going to email the IT help desk.
15. Kelly is going to email the sales department.
16. Kelly is going to speak to the director.
17. Kelly is going to speak to the IT help desk.
18. Kelly is going to speak to the sales department.

45.4

1 False
2 Not given
3 False
4 True
5 False

45.5 Model Answers

1 Paul is going to contact the presenters.
2 Paul is going to ask the printers for ten extra copies of the training booklets.
3 The printers are going to supply name badges in the form of lanyards.
4 Marie is going to meet the presenters.
5 The presenters will get to the venue by taxi.
6 Omar is going to check that the venue will cater for people with special dietary requirements.

46

46.1 🔊

1 text message
2 website
3 stamp
4 voicemail
5 conference call
6 email
7 bulletin board (US) / notice board (UK)
8 letter
9 internal mail
10 mail (US) / post (UK)
11 web conference
12 presentation
13 transfer a call
14 envelope
15 social networking

46.2 🔊
1 attachment
2 forward
3 trash
4 signature
5 outbox
6 print
7 reply all
8 inbox
9 subject

46.3 🔊
1 TBC
2 BCC
3 RE
4 CC
5 FYI
6 ETA
7 NB
8 ASAP

47

47.1 🔊
1 I work **in** the finance department at Forrester's.
2 Please confirm your availability **ASAP**.
3 Please find your **receipt attached** to this email.
4 Please **don't hesitate** to contact me.
5 I am writing **with reference to** invoice number 146.
6 Please see the agenda **attached** here.
7 I work in the IT department **at** Transtech.
8 I **am** writing to invite you to a meeting next week.
9 Please **don't** hesitate to contact me.
10 Please return your signed contract **ASAP**.
11 I **would** be grateful if you could get back to me soon.
12 I am writing **with** regard to your complaint.
13 Please find the minutes **attached** here.
14 I would **be** grateful if we could arrange a meeting.
15 I work **in** the company's catering department.
16 I am the new Head of Sales **at** Codequote.
17 I am writing with regard **to** our schedule.
18 Please let me know if you **have** any questions.
19 Please **find** the new designs attached here.

47.2 🔊
1 I am writing with regard to your latest feedback.
2 Please find the invoice attached here.
3 I would be grateful if you could pay the outstanding invoice.
4 If you have any questions, please do not hesitate to contact me.

47.3 🔊
1 I am writing with **regard to our invoice number AB3168**.
2 I work in **the accounts department at Shuberg's**.
3 I would be grateful if you **could let us know when you have been paid**.
4 I deal with **the supply and payment of invoices**.
5 It has come to our attention **that invoice DY895 has not been paid**.
6 I wonder if **you are aware that we have not been paid**.
7 I am writing to **inform you that we are going to use a new supplier**.

47.4 🔊
1 He **is giving** all the candidates a task to do before their interview.
2 We **are meeting** other suppliers on Tuesday.
3 Sam **is going to make** coffee for the CEO's visitors.
4 Carlos **is presenting** the sales figures tomorrow.
5 We **are going to discuss** sales figures for the last quarter.
6 They **are giving** all their clients a voucher.
7 He **is going to travel** to Italy to meet the new CEO.
8 Greg **is going to pack** all the boxes into the delivery van.
9 A famous hairdresser **is going to open** the new salon.
10 We **are launching** the new company logo at the sales conference.
11 The company **is going to recycle** all the stationery with the old logo.

47.5 🔊
1 I am writing with regard to the shareholders' meeting on Thursday.
2 We are meeting new clients at the Radcliffe Hotel.
3 The meeting is taking place in the hotel's conference center.
4 We are going to discuss the last quarter's sales figures.
5 The new CEO is taking questions after his presentation.
6 He is going to discuss the company's future marketing strategy.

47.6
3

Acknowledgments

The publisher would like to thank:
Amy Child, Dominic Clifford, Devika Khosla, and Priyansha Tuli for design assistance; Dominic Clifford and Hansa Babra for additional illustrations; Sam Atkinson, Vineetha Mokkil, Antara Moitra, Margaret Parrish, Nisha Shaw, and Rohan Sinha for editorial assistance; Elizabeth Wise for indexing; Jo Kent for additional text; Scarlett O'Hara, Georgina Palffy, and Helen Ridge for proofreading; Christine Stroyan for project management; ID Audio for audio recording and production; David Almond, Gillian Reid, and Jacqueline Street-Elkayam for production assistance.

DK would like to thank the following for their kind permission to use their photograph:
33 **123RF.com**: Federico Rostagno / ilfede (top left)
All other images © Dorling Kindersley Limited.